ISSUES THAT CONCERN YOU

Attention Deficit Hyperactivity Disorder

Heidi Watkins, *Book Editor*

GREENHAVEN PRESS
A part of Gale, Cengage Learning

GALE
CENGAGE Learning™

Detroit • New York • San Francisco • New Haven, Conn • Waterville, Maine • London

GALE
CENGAGE Learning™

Christine Nasso, *Publisher*
Elizabeth Des Chenes, *Managing Editor*

© 2011 Greenhaven Press, a part of Gale, Cengage Learning

Gale and Greenhaven Press are registered trademarks used herein under license.

For more information, contact:
Greenhaven Press
27500 Drake Rd.
Farmington Hills, MI 48331-3535
Or you can visit our Internet site at gale.cengage.com

For product information and technology assistance, contact us at

Gale Customer Support, 1-800-877-4253
For permission to use material from this text or product, submit all requests online at www.cengage.com/permissions

Further permissions questions can be e-mailed to permissionrequest@cengage.com

Articles in Greenhaven Press anthologies are often edited for length to meet page requirements. In addition, original titles of these works are changed to clearly present the main thesis and to explicitly indicate the author's opinion. Every effort is made to ensure that Greenhaven Press accurately reflects the original intent of the authors. Every effort has been made to trace the owners of copyrighted material.

LIBRARY OF CONGRESS CATALOGING-IN-PUBLICATION DATA

Attention deficit hyperactivity disorder / Heidi Watkins, book editor.
    p. cm. -- (Issues that concern you)
  Includes bibliographical references and index.
  ISBN 978-0-7377-4950-2 (hardcover)
  1. Attention-deficit hyperactivity disorder. I. Watkins, Heidi.
  RJ506.H9A926 2010
  618.92'8589--dc22
                                                                    2010013958

Printed in the United States of America
1 2 3 4 5 6 7 14 13 12 11 10

CONTENTS

Attention deficit hyperactivity disorder (ADHD) is one of the most common mental health disorders affecting children and teens. In fact, it is likely that in an average classroom in the United States, at least one or two students have ADHD, which is most commonly associated with symptoms like difficulty sitting still, having trouble taking turns, or frequently interrupting others. Like most disorders, however, ADHD is complex and multifaceted. It does not manifest itself in the same way for everyone, and some of the ways that it shows up may be rather unexpected.

One of the more recently studied manifestations of ADHD is Internet addiction. Internet addiction is fairly prevalent, affecting 8 to 13 percent of college undergraduates, according to one study. Addiction to the Internet may be a parent's first warning sign that ADHD is present.

Internet addiction is a relatively recent development. Although it is not an officially recognized diagnosis listed in the most recent edition of the *Diagnostic and Statistical Manual of Mental Disorders*, the inclusion of Internet addiction disorder (IAD) is under consideration for the 2012 edition.

For working purposes, researchers often use the following diagnostic criteria published by Kimberly S. Young in 1998:

- A preoccupation with the Internet
- A need to use the Internet for increasing amounts of time for the same amount of satisfaction
- An inability to reduce Internet use
- Feelings of irritability or depression when trying to reduce Internet use
- Staying online longer than planned
- Risking educational or job opportunities or personal relationships due to excessive Internet use

- Lying to others to hide the extent of Internet use
- Using the Internet as a means of escaping from feelings or problems

Some cases of Internet addiction can be severe. In one case report, two psychiatrists describe a fifteen-year-old who spent twelve to eighteen hours a day online and up to thirty-eight hours uninterruptedly. For two years he did not go to school; furthermore, on three occasions he assaulted his mother when she unplugged his computer. Finally, he was hospitalized. In this severe case, the teen did have ADHD, but he also had other severe mental disorders, including obsessive-compulsive disorder and bipolar disorder. In another extreme case, a twenty-year-old South Korean man collapsed and died after playing the online role-playing game *Starcraft* for fifty hours with very few breaks. He also recently had been fired from his job for missing too much work because of his gaming addiction.

Internet addiction is a serious matter. It can range from a preoccupation with the Internet to complete obsession with it. It can damage school and work performance, negatively affect family and other personal relationships, and also heighten depression in children and teens. It is also associated with additional problems. One study says that it may be one explanation for sleep disorders in children and teens with ADHD, and another study, although it does not mention ADHD, does establish a link between Internet addiction and self-harm in teens, such as cutting.

The connection between ADHD and Internet addiction has been well established in recent years by reliable clinical studies. One study, appearing in the October 2009 *Archives of Pediatric and Adolescent Medicine*, followed more than two thousand students from ten junior high schools in Taiwan and found that teens with ADHD were more likely to be addicted to the Internet than other teens and were most likely to spend their time online gaming and chatting.

Another 2009 study, this one appearing in *CyberPsychology & Behavior*, examined ADHD and Internet addiction among college students, particularly looking at gender differences and assessing which of three ADHD factors were most present in those who

Internet addiction is a serious matter. Here a young Internet addict in China receives treatment for his addiction at a government facility in Beijing.

were addicted: attention deficit, hyperactivity, or impulsivity. The study found that attention deficit was the most present symptom of those addicted to the Internet and that the association between attention deficit and Internet addiction was strongest among the women.

The studies offer several explanations for the link between Internet addiction and ADHD. One is simply that those with ADHD, especially the inattentive type, are easily bored and the online environment provides instant feedback and reward as well as the opportunity for multiple windows of activity taking place at the same time. Another, perhaps related, possibility is that people with ADHD crave the dopamine that is released into their brain with Internet use; in other words, Internet addiction is a kind of self-medication. A study mentioned in the June 2009 issue of the *Brown University Child and Adolescent Psychopharmacology Update* followed children with both ADHD and Internet video game addiction who were prescribed the drug methylphenidate, which increases dopamine levels in the brain. At the end of the eight-week study, the children showed a significant decrease in both ADHD symptoms and time spent on the Internet, suggesting dopamine craving as the cause of Internet addiction.

Attention deficit hyperactivity disorder is a complicated condition and a significant problem. It is a matter worthy of discussion for professionals as well as today's students. The articles in *Issues That Concern You: Attention Deficit Hyperactivity Disorder* represent multiple viewpoints regarding the condition. In addition, the volume contains several appendixes to help the reader understand and explore the topic, including a thorough bibliography and a list of organizations to contact for further information. The appendix titled "What You Should Know About Attention Deficit Hyperactivity Disorder" offers facts about ADHD, including prevalence, diagnosis, causes, and treatment. The appendix "What You Should Do About Attention Deficit Hyperactivity Disorder" offers tips for young people afflicted with ADHD and ways to help a friend or family member with the disorder. With all these features, this volume provides a detailed resource for those interested in this issue.

ONE

Teens with ADHD Face Special Problems

National Resource Center on AD/HD

> Living with ADHD is not easy for anyone, and being a teenager is not easy either. The combination—being a teen with ADHD—poses unique challenges. The following viewpoint from the What We Know series, published by the National Resource Center on AD/HD, was written especially for teenagers with ADHD. The article provides information on conditions such as anxiety disorders and substance abuse, for which teens with ADHD are at special risk; discusses areas of a teen's life that ADHD can affect, such as academic performance and family life; outlines different management and treatment options for ADHD; and touches on additional issues, such as driving.

"I have AD/HD . . . so what??" In many ways, "so what" is right: mostly, you are just a regular teen, with all the ups and downs that come with being a teenager. In other ways, growing up and heading towards adulthood with AD/HD (attention-deficit/hyperactivity disorder) presents some unique challenges and obstacles. People used to think that just young kids had AD/HD, something that you grew out of as you got older. Now we know differently. Today's research has shown that most kids

National Resource Center on AD/HD, "AD/HD and Teens: Information for Teens," 2008. Reproduced by permission.

do not outgrow AD/HD when they reach adolescence, and most teens don't outgrow AD/HD when they become young adults. So what does being a teen with AD/HD really mean?

First, you should know that having AD/HD doesn't have to get in the way of living the life you want. Countless teens just like you have grown up to pursue their passions, live happy lives, and be successful in their work. They've found this success because they've taken the time to learn how AD/HD affects them and taken charge of a treatment plan that works for them and their unique situation.

"I'm Not a Kid Anymore"— AD/HD in the Teen Years

The main symptoms required for a diagnosis of AD/HD— inattention, hyperactivity, and impulsivity—remain the same during your teens as they were earlier in your childhood. However, you may notice some differences. For example, you may struggle less with symptoms of hyperactivity (such as fidgeting or staying seated) now than you did when you were younger. On the other hand, you may notice greater challenges with staying on top of your schoolwork and other responsibilities. This is because there are more demands on your time and higher expectations for you to function independently now that you are a teen. This can all feel overwhelming, but don't worry—these challenges are not that different from what your friends are going through whether they have AD/HD or not. In your case, it may be more pronounced, but proper treatment can help you adjust as you grow into yourself and adjust to the changes in your life.

Another characteristic associated with AD/HD in adolescence is difficulty with "executive functioning." This term refers to the functions within the brain that [according to ADHD researcher T. E. Brown], "activate, organize, integrate, and manage other functions." In other words, executive function allows you to think about goals and consequences for your actions, plan accordingly, evaluate your progress, and shift plans as necessary. Sound familiar? This may be exactly what your parents and teachers have been trying to help you with over the years. However, in adolescence, your parents and teachers expect you to start doing these things more independently, and sometimes that transition can be tough on you and those around you.

"Why Me?"—Causes of AD/HD

You may wonder why you have AD/HD. Some teens feel guilty for having AD/HD. Others feel that it is something that they should be able to control on their own or be cured of. Having AD/HD is not your fault! Research has clearly shown that AD/HD runs in families and is highly genetic. AD/HD is a brain-based disorder, and the symptoms shown in AD/HD are linked to many specific brain areas. There is no known "cure" for AD/HD, but we know many things that can minimize the impact AD/HD has on your everyday life.

"Is It Just AD/HD?"—Other Conditions in the Teen Years

Some teens with AD/HD also have the challenge of other conditions that are common with AD/HD. These conditions may have been present since you were much younger, or may emerge with the additional stress of adolescence. The fact is that up to 60% of children and teens with AD/HD have been found to have at least one other condition, so don't think you're alone.

- Some of the other conditions commonly experienced by teens with AD/HD may affect how you act and have names that may sound pretty heavy. Specific ones include Oppositional Defiant Disorder (ODD) and Conduct Disorder (CD). ODD is a term that means you may have difficulty accepting and following the rules and limits set by authority figures. CD is more severe and includes having difficulty with following rules set by authority figures but also includes difficulty following rules and laws set by society.
- Other conditions that affect how you feel (called mood disorders), including depression and dysthymia (a type of

Teens with ADHD have a much higher risk of substance abuse.

negative mood similar to depression but that lasts longer),
can also be common in teens with AD/HD. Bipolar disorder is another type of mood disorder. However, a diagnosis
of bipolar disorder in teens is controversial and a diagnosis
of AD/HD does not appear to increase the risk for bipolar
disorder.
- Anxiety disorders may be present in as many as 10–40%
of teens with AD/HD. Anxiety disorders are characterized
by excessive worry, difficulty controlling your worries, and
physical symptoms including headaches or upset stomach.

They can also include "anxiety attacks" and make you want to avoid situations that make you anxious.

- Substance use and abuse is a significant concern of many parents and teens. The risk for later substance use among children with AD/HD ranges from 12–24%. Some substances (like alcohol) may be illegal for you based on your age. Other substances (like marijuana or other drugs) may be illegal, period! For these reasons alone you should avoid using them. If you choose to use such substances and find you have difficulty controlling yourself, if others have expressed concerns to you about your use, if you need the substance to "get going" or "slow down," or if you feel guilty about your use, you may have a substance problem. You should get professional help from a licensed mental health professional or addiction specialist.
- Learning and communication problems can also be common and may become apparent with the added demands of middle school and high school. If you are concerned about your ability to learn in the classroom, your ability to understand what others say to you, or your ability to express yourself the way you want to, then you should tell your parent(s). You may need an evaluation by a professional to determine how you learn, think, or communicate.
- Sleep disturbance is also common in teens with AD/HD. Changes in sleep cycles are normal for all teens and you may have noticed that you prefer to stay up later at night, sleep later in the morning, and need more sleep overall. As a teen with AD/HD, you may have difficulty sleeping well and this may not necessarily be a side effect of medications.

At this time, it is not possible to predict who will experience these additional difficulties. It is likely that genetics play a role. The additional stresses experienced by some teens with AD/HD, such as social criticism or internal frustration, may also make you more vulnerable to these difficulties. . . .

What should you do if you suspect that you may suffer from any of these additional disorders? Talk to your parent(s) about getting an evaluation by a psychologist, psychiatrist, or other trained mental health professional.

"My Life with AD/HD"

What does it feel like to have AD/HD? You may experience stigma or embarrassment related to your diagnosis. You may also wish to deny that you have AD/HD. Having AD/HD may make you feel different from your friends and you may want to believe that your symptoms have lessened or even disappeared. It is important for you to understand that you are not responsible for having AD/HD. Having AD/HD is not due to any mistake you made and is not a punishment. AD/HD is just like other medical conditions, such as asthma or poor eyesight. You can't control the fact that you have AD/HD, but you can control the way you manage it. Following your treatment plan is a key to meeting your goals and achieving success.

You may have difficulty feeling good about yourself or you may feel that you are not as good as your friends or other students. Research shows that teens with AD/HD and learning disabilities report feeling severely stressed when going to school and sitting in class, feeling tired, having frequent arguments with close friends, feeling different from other classmates, having low self-esteem, and feeling that their parents didn't understand them. If you feel this way, remember, you are not alone and you can feel better. Talk with a parent, another trusted adult, or health professional about how you feel. Participate in activities you enjoy and recognize that everyone has different strengths and weaknesses.

Many teens are concerned about talking with their friends about their AD/HD. You may feel that your friends don't understand your difficulties or may make fun of you. You can choose the friends with whom to discuss your AD/HD and what details you want to share. However, explaining AD/HD to your trusted friends may surprise you—they may be a great source of support, or even have AD/HD themselves! Although the exact number of children and adolescents with AD/HD is unclear, somewhere be-

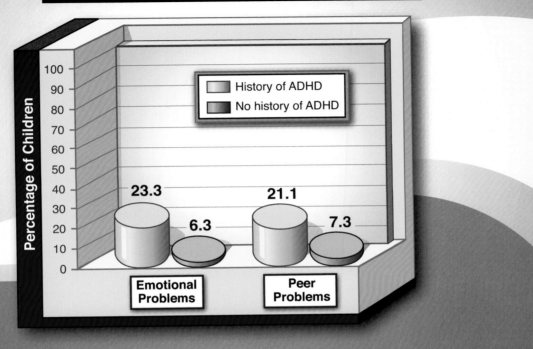

Emotional and Peer Problems Among Teens and Children Aged Four to Seventeen with and Without ADHD

Percentage of Children

- History of ADHD
- No history of ADHD

23.3 · 6.3 — Emotional Problems

21.1 · 7.3 — Peer Problems

Taken from: Tara W. Strine et al., "Emotional and Behavioral Difficulties and Impairments in Everyday Functioning Among Children with a History of Attention-Deficit/Hyperactivity Disorder," *Preventing Chronic Disease*, vol. 3, no. 2, April 2006. www.cdc.gov/pcd/issues/2006/apr/05_0171.htm.

tween 1.4 million and 2.3 million youths have AD/HD, so you are far from alone in facing the challenges that come with it.

AD/HD Can Affect Many Aspects of Life

- *Academic performance.* High school students' lives are more hectic, with more demands to juggle, and less supervision. Academically, the workload and difficulty of the material increases, and long-term projects rather than daily homework assignments are the norm. These factors all present challenges to teens with AD/HD. You may benefit from assistance with note-taking, study skills, and organization/time management. As you develop these skills, you will come to rely less on parents or teachers and be more confident about your own ability to structure your time and perform at your potential. Students who have a diagnosis of AD/HD and whose AD/HD symptoms impair their academic functioning may qualify for classroom accommodations. These accommodations are based on your particular needs, but can include extra time on tests, taking tests in a separate location where distractions are minimized, or additional organizational support. Work with your parents and your school if you think you might need and want this kind of help.

- *Social functioning.* In adolescence, your relationships with others your age become increasingly important to you. But these relationships are not always easy to navigate! During these years, your friendships are changing, you become interested in dating, and you encounter more significant peer pressure. You may notice that you tend to be more easily frustrated or more emotionally sensitive than others your age—this is common for teens with AD/HD. Some teens with AD/HD have no difficulty establishing and maintaining relationships, while others find negotiating different personalities, expectations, and desires quite challenging. Participating in structured social activities, such as sports, clubs, or youth groups, can help provide you with a built in social group and shared positive experiences.

- *Home functioning.* Nearly every teenager has conflict with his or her parents over rules, privileges, household chores, friends . . . you name it! However, on average, households of adolescents with AD/HD have higher levels of parent-teen conflict than households with adolescents who do not have AD/HD. Why is this the case? One source of conflict in the home is that teens want more freedom and independence. However, the difficulties with organization, forgetfulness, and thinking before acting that commonly go along with AD/HD may make your parent(s) reluctant to give you the freedom you desire. In addition, many teens with AD/HD have more difficulty completing homework and chores on time or following other rules due to inattention, distractibility, lack of interest, or lack of organization. This can be frustrating for both you and your parent(s), and may lead to a cycle of negative interaction. In such a cycle, your parent(s) may lecture, yell, or punish and you may respond with anger, or other ways that aren't very helpful. As this occurs repeatedly, more minor demands on the part of your parent(s) and more minor lack of compliance with rules or requests on your part can trigger the escalation of negativity. *What can be done to interrupt this cycle?* Clear communication is always important, and discussing issues when you are angry is never effective. Instead, set aside a time when all parties are calm to discuss any areas of disagreement or conflict. If family conflict is taking a large toll on the family, you and your parents may consider seeking help from qualified mental health professional.

"So What Can I Do About It?"— Treatment of AD/HD

You already know that no cure currently exists for AD/HD. This doesn't mean that there's nothing you can do about it! While there is no cure, many people just like you have had great success with the current treatments available. The focus of these treatments is symptom management. Although the symptoms of AD/HD may change with age, you may still require treatment to target these symptoms and even may need such treatment into adulthood.

Education is a necessary component to any effective treatment plan and provides you with the tools to understand your disorder and how to manage it. If you were diagnosed with AD/HD when you were very young, it is likely that this education was directed to your parent(s). It is important that you receive this education as well, ask your doctors and treatment providers questions, and express concerns if you have them. However, education is only one component of a successful plan to treat AD/HD, and medication and behavioral therapy can be used as well.

It is a myth that medication becomes less effective in the teen years. In fact, medications should be as effective, but patterns of co-occurring conditions may require changes to the treatment regimen. You and your parent(s) may also consider a change to a long acting medication to provide you with better symptom management throughout the day, as you may have activities after the school day has ended and into the evening hours. . . .

Behavioral treatment is another common treatment approach for teens with AD/HD. Proven psychosocial treatments include parent-teen training in problem-solving and communication skills, parent training in behavioral management methods, and teacher training in classroom management. . . .

Little or no research currently exists to support the use of dietary treatments, traditional psychotherapy, play therapy, cognitive behavioral therapy, or social skills training. However, these interventions may be effective in treating co-occurring conditions if present. . . .

The most common treatment for teens with AD/HD likely combines medication and psychosocial treatment. This is known as multi-modal treatment.

"What Else Do I Need to Know?"— Additional Issues for Teens with AD/HD

As a teen with AD/HD, you are facing the same issues that prove challenging for your peers: developing your identity, establishing your independence, understanding your emerging sexuality, making choices regarding drugs and alcohol, and setting goals for your future. However, you may also face some unique difficulties, as described below.

- *Driving.* Getting your driver's license is an exciting event, and one that indicates increased freedom and independence. However, inattention and impulsivity can lead to difficulties with driving. Drivers with AD/HD have more tickets, are involved in more accidents, make more impulsive errors, and have slower and more variable reaction times. The use of stimulant medications has been found to have positive effects on driving performance. Always follow safe driving habits, such as using a seat-belt, observing the speed limit, and minimizing distractions such as the use of mobile phones and eating while driving.

- *Adherence to medication regimen.* Nearly half of children don't take their medications as prescribed, and the use of AD/HD medications decreases over the teenage years. This occurs for a multitude of reasons: you may have negative attitudes towards medication use, you may feel that your AD/HD symptoms are not impairing your functioning, you may dislike the side effects of the medication, or you may simply want to "take a vacation" from your medications to see what happens. If you and your parents decide to discontinue your use of medication, you should consult with your physician and designate a "trial period" for doing so. During this period, you should specify your goals and develop a plan to achieve those goals. Your plan may include tutors or frequent check-ins with a teacher or counselor. Make sure to specify what indicators might illustrate the need for re-starting the medication (such as declining grades or increases in conflict at home). After a time, evaluate your progress with your parent(s) and your physician and determine whether or not medication is effective for you.

- *Diversion of medications.* Use or abuse of AD/HD medicines among individuals for whom these medications are not prescribed is an increasing problem. Individuals who use non-prescription stimulants may do so for either academic reasons (improving their ability to study or succeed on tests) or for recreational reasons (to get a high or a buzz). At some point in your life, friends or acquaintances may ask you to give or sell your medications to them for these purposes. The use of medications by individuals for whom they were not prescribed is illegal and could have serious legal consequences. In addition, your AD/HD medications are safe and effective when taken as directed, but can be dangerous if used without medical supervision. You should never give or sell medications that are prescribed to you to anyone else. Take some time to think about how you might respond if someone asks you for these medications. Would you . . . change the subject? . . . simply refuse and walk away? . . . explain the dangers of non-prescription medication use? . . . tell them that your parents monitor your pills and would notice if some were missing? It is likely that you will face this situation and being prepared with your response is important.

- *Building your self-esteem.* Living with AD/HD can be challenging. Many teens with AD/HD find that the school environment does not suit their personality or maximize their natural talents. It is important for you to find your niche and identify your strengths: Are you athletic? A good artist? Do you have musical talent? Are you good with computers? Find environments and activities that remind you of your strengths and allow you to experience success. Remind yourself that everyone has strengths and weakness. The important thing is to do your best to work through difficulties and spend plenty of time on activities in which you shine.

"What About My Future?"

The answer is, only you can determine what lies in store for you and your future. The fact that you are taking the time to read this information . . . and educate yourself about your diagnosis shows that you are reflecting on your strengths and weaknesses and taking steps to prepare yourself for your future. We know that teens with AD/HD are at risk for potentially serious problems as they transition into adulthood. We also know that as many as two-thirds of teens with AD/HD continue to experience significant symptoms of AD/HD in adulthood. In addition, as they become adults, teens with AD/HD are at higher risk for difficulties in education, occupation, and social relationships. However, these are only risks, they are not guarantees. Most teens with AD/HD become successful, productive adults—and so can you! Continued awareness and treatment is crucial so that you can avoid the risks and meet the goals you set for yourself— whatever they are!

TWO

ADHD Has Lost Much of Its Stigma

Lindsey Frank

> Despite the prevalence of ADHD, until recent years the disorder has been poorly understood and underdiagnosed. Its sufferers have been stigmatized, and they have struggled in many areas of life, particularly education. In this viewpoint Lindsey Frank, a reporter for McClatchy-Tribune Information Services, interviews people with ADHD from three different generations, including an eighty-year-old, a fifty-three-year-old, and two young college students. Their conversations reveal the extreme differences in acceptance and treatment options from the early twentieth century until now. Frank also explains current mandates giving students diagnosed with ADHD the legal right to educational accommodations, such as instructional modifications and extra time on exams.

Donna Love always had trouble in school.

She knew she was bright, but something consistently prevented her from succeeding. She had trouble organizing her time, often blurted things out in class and always felt isolated. She eventually dropped out of college after receiving bad grades, spent decades living without a college degree, and then went back to school in her 50s to earn a college diploma. She then attempted graduate school a few years later, only to drop out after once again struggling with academics.

Love, 80, always knew she was different from her peers, but never knew why.

Until 12 years ago.

A Mystery Solved

When Love was 68, she was working as a psychological assistant, and encountered a client who had Attention Deficit Hyperactivity Disorder. After listening to the client's symptoms, and realizing they seemed all-too familiar, she decided to get tested for the disorder herself. A doctor confirmed her suspicion, and suddenly all of Love's struggles made sense.

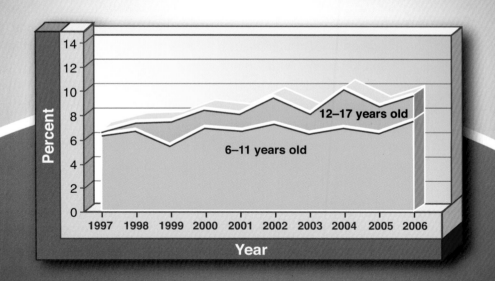

All Diagnoses of ADHD Among U.S. Teens and Children, by Age Group, 1997–2006

12–17 years old

6–11 years old

Taken from: P.N. Pastor and C.A. Reuben, "Diagnosed Attention Deficit Hyperactivity Disorder and Learning Disability: United States," 2004–2006, National Center for Health Statistics, *Vital Health Stat*, 2008.

"Growing up, I had never even heard of ADHD," said Love, who now receives medical treatment and has learned behavioral management techniques to combat the symptoms of the disorder. She also works as a mentor for people who have ADHD and founded an adult ADHD support group.

ADHD is a common neurobiological condition that affects more than four million people in the United States. University of California, Berkeley psychology department chair Stephen Hinshaw, Ph.D., who has studied ADHD for more than 25 years, says the condition is characterized by distractibility, impulsivity and hyperactivity on one hand, and by intelligence, creativity and energy on the other.

A New Understanding

While the symptoms of ADHD remain the same, the perception of it has changed greatly over time. When Love was young, ADHD was called "minimal brain dysfunction." The condition was under-diagnosed and was thought to be the result of laziness and poor parenting, said Bryan Goodman, director of communications for Children and Adults with Attention Deficit/Hyperactivity Disorder (CHADD). Now, as people and organizations make efforts to educate people about ADHD and reduce its negative stigma, there has been a societal shift in how it is perceived—making it much easier for people who have the disorder to cope.

Love, though currently receiving treatment and able to cope with her disorder, feels her academic setbacks stopped her from living up to her potential. Her story differs from that of many young people today, who have received treatment for and learned to overcome the symptoms of ADHD since an early age.

Two such young people are University of California, Berkeley sophomore Blake Taylor and Sheridan (Wyoming) College junior Courtney Gifford. Taylor is a molecular and cell biology and French literature double major, and the author of the memoir *ADHD & Me: What I Learned from Lighting Fires at the Dinner Table* (New Harbinger, $14.95). Gifford is a 4.0 student, and the reigning Miss Wyoming, with a platform of ADD and ADHD.

Early Struggles

But life has not always been easy for these two students, who, like Love, have encountered many obstacles as a result of ADHD.

Taylor recalls having an especially hard time controlling his impulses as a child—a common symptom of the disorder. He remembers one afternoon, when he was sitting in the kitchen with his sister (who also has ADHD), she began lighting a yogurt container on fire. Wondering what would happen if he put something flammable on the fire, Blake retrieved eye drops and poured them on the lighted container.

"It blew up immediately," Taylor said. "There was fire all over the table . . . rug . . . chairs." . . .

In hindsight, Taylor knows his actions were wrong. He explains he was not trying to be bad, "it was more out of curiosity," he said. "Curiosity is often mistranslated into people with ADHD being bad."

Gifford did not "act out" as much as Taylor (typically girls and boys manifest their symptoms in different ways, she said), but she does recall having mood swings, excessive amounts of energy and being very forgetful as a child.

An Early Diagnosis

Both Taylor and Gifford were diagnosed with ADHD at age 5, and have been receiving medical and psychological treatment ever since. They were born into a generation when people began to research and understand ADHD. New studies and tests have shown it has a strong neurological basis, according to the Web site for CHADD. These new studies, in combination with the creation of CHADD in 1987, have opened doors to the paradigm shift that has begun to take place in public perceptions of ADHD.

"If (Blake and Courtney) had grown up in the 80s, they would be reluctant to be so upfront and open about having ADHD," Goodman said. "They would have struggled a lot more in school because, while schools would have acknowledged other disorders, it would have been up in the air as to whether ADHD would be accommodated. I think it would be much

Because guidelines for diagnosing ADHD did not exist until 1987, many adults who had the disorder as children remained undiagnosed.

harder for them to be the kind of role models they are and be so open about their ADHD."

Lew Mills, 53, is a psychotherapist who works with adults who have been diagnosed with ADHD, and was himself diagnosed with the disorder as an adult. He spent his school years being frustrated with his inability to focus on and complete tasks, and finally got tested for the disorder while trying to finish his dissertation for his PhD—a task that proved exceedingly difficult. Originally diagnosed with anxiety/depression and put on anti-depressants, Mills was diagnosed with ADHD in 1996. At the time, finishing his dissertation, "all of the sudden happened," he said. "I got back to having a career and having my life in place. It just made everything easier."

Though ADHD was first referenced in 1845 (when German physician Heinrich Hoffman wrote a poem that included a character named "Fidgety Phil"), the term ADHD did not exist until 1987, when it was published in the *Diagnostic and Statistical Manual of Mental Disorders*.

Limited Acceptance

In the early 1990s, many people were still reluctant to associate themselves with ADHD. Others did not believe ADHD was an actual disorder. When Taylor was diagnosed in 1994, he said his mother was the only person who believed ADHD was a real problem.

"My dad and my grandparents were against me going to a psychiatrist and taking medication," Taylor said. "ADHD had a stigma attached to it. They were against me being diagnosed with something they didn't really believe existed."

Taylor said early in his diagnosis there were even some teachers who did not accept ADHD.

Educational Support

To correct the misconceptions about ADHD and mandate fair treatment of students with the disorder, CHADD sought legal protection for ADHD students. In 1991, as a result of CHADD's efforts, the U.S. Department of Education issued a Policy Clarification Memorandum directing schools to include ADHD as a covered disability under the Individuals With Disabilities Education Act. As a result of this resolution, students with ADHD are eligible for special accommodation—options people from older generations, like Mills and Love, never had.

Most accommodations involve classroom structure and instructional modifications, explained Mary Sherry, a Maryland middle and high school psychologist, who works with students with ADHD. Students with ADHD are placed closer to the point of instruction and/or away from distractions. Some students are also given cubicles, instead of the typical desk. Instructors are taught to recognize when students with ADHD are going off track, and cue the students to begin paying attention. Instructors also work with students to help organize their work and plan their time, through the use of planners and calendars, Sherry said.

Taylor has taken advantage of these accommodations throughout his schooling, and feels they have aided him in his success. He receives 50-percent extra time on tests, and is permitted to work in a separate quiet room, where he is able to concentrate and spread out his work. Taylor says his teachers in high school and college have been especially helpful, something he attributes to the shift in society's perception of ADHD since the 1990s.

Gifford also has taken advantage of the accommodations, and has maintained a 4.0 GPA during her time at Sheridan—a difficult task for anyone with a learning disability. "I'm one of the people who can break the mold," she said. "I set my standards high."

Other Interventions

Accommodations in schools are not the only way to assist students with ADHD. Treating the disorder often requires medical, educational, behavioral and psychological intervention, according to the U.S. Department of Health and Human Services Web site. This comprehensive approach to treatment is called "multimodal" and may include parent training, behavioral intervention strategies, education regarding ADHD and medication.

Though there have been huge strides taken, there is still a long path to eliminating the negative stigma often attached to the disorder. Taylor had a classmate say he faked ADHD to get extra time on the SATs, and Gifford has had peers suggest students with the disorder can't do well in school.

"There have been a lot of changes. Some are positive—we now recognize that ADHD is real, that it can cause a lot of very real and very problematic impairments, and that it can be managed and treated (if not, as of yet, cured)," Berkeley's Hinshaw said. "At the same time, the spate of negative publicity coupled with the general stigma of mental illness and the critiques of medication treatment, make it a controversial topic."

Awareness Through Education

Taylor, Gifford and CHADD's Goodman all agree that the way to reduce the negative stigma of ADHD is to continue educating people about the disorder, by creating awareness and alleviating negative stereotypes.

Despite the difficulties, Taylor still calls ADHD his "special gift," because he has so much extra energy to put into his work—energy that others do not have. "When I was younger my mom told me I 'have a Ferrari engine . . . it's very fast but you have to learn to control it.'"

While young people like Taylor have had their whole lives to learn to control their ADHD, Love is just beginning the struggle. When presented with Taylor's description of ADHD as a "special gift," she said he is one of the fortunate people.

"(Taylor) must have had some good parenting and support along the way," she said, referring to assistance from his family members and teachers—support she did not have.

Nonetheless, Love is grateful to finally know what has caused her difficulties throughout the years. "Not only can I help myself, but I can help other adults . . . which is something I wouldn't have been able to do if I hadn't figured out what my problem was," she said. "It just shows the possibilities that open when someone finally does get help."

THREE

ADHD Diagnosis and Medication Are Harmful to Children

Douglas P. Olsen and Susan Froetschel

The son of Douglas P. Olsen, an associate professor at Yale School of Nursing, and Susan Froetschel, a professional writer, was a second-grader who had trouble sitting still. His teacher recommended medication, and when the parents did not medicate their son, the teacher put his desk in the hallway outside of the classroom. They wrote a column about it, and when a national news program investigated the situation, they found that ten other kids in the boy's second-grade class were taking ADHD medication. The following viewpoint, an opinion piece for the *Richmond (VA) Times-Dispatch*, is a ten-year follow-up from their original opinion piece, revealing how their son succeeded and graduated from high school without medication. Olsen and Froetschel assert that teachers and parents should resist the urge to label a child as having ADHD. For those children suspected of having ADHD, the authors maintain, medication should be a last resort. Instead, parents and teachers should develop strategies that help such young people cope with their challenges and achieve success.

Ten years ago in the face of unceasing pressure from our son's school, we wrote an Op/Ed column ("Here's No. 1 Abused

Drug in Our Elementary Schools") about our battle with Henrico's public schools. As a second-grader, our son squirmed in his chair, spoke out of turn, and scribbled his sentences. He was pulled out of classes for special education. His teacher predicted poor test scores if we didn't try medication, and recommended a pediatrician who would prescribe the drug.

We hesitated, and the teacher placed our son's desk in the hallway, where he read *Goosebumps* for most of that year. ABC'S news program, "20/20," read our opinion column and investigated. At least 10 of the children in the second-grade classroom were on stimulant medication for ADD or ADHD.

In our column, we wrote: "We reluctantly agree that the drug probably makes the job of a frazzled teacher in a crowded classroom much easier. But at what price? How much creativity are we destroying? How much self-discipline?

"Is the goal of Virginia's public education system to create conformity among students or allow individual potential to thrive? As parents, we oppose the trend toward quick fixes to solve problems, widespread medication to young children, and efforts to make that medication easier to obtain."

Some experts say that teachers and parents may be too quick to label a child as having ADHD.

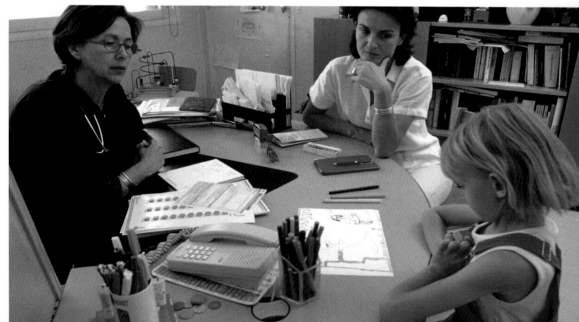

The district refused alternatives such as more discipline, changing teachers, or changing schools. So we ended up moving away from the Richmond area after that one school year.

Success Without Medication

Ten years later, with no medication, Nick made it to his senior year in high school. Still physically restless, he thrives academically and socially. Captain of the track team and finalist at the state science fair, he scored above 1400 on the SAT and ranked third in his class. He does community service and has held summer jobs requiring meticulous research skills.

Virginia and other states have taken the wise step of passing legislation that curbs the tendency of some teachers to "diagnose" children with behavior problems. Yet too many teachers and parents continue to rely on diagnoses to label children, limiting educational opportunities. Children labeled with ADD or ADHD quickly learn that adults expect them to squirm, perform poorly on tests, and misbehave.

Any diagnosis of ADD or ADHD should remain suspect, and medication should be a last resort. There is no objective test for the disorder. Like all psychiatric diagnoses, it requires making judgments about the child's behavior. Teachers often initiate the diagnostic process, and the diagnosis depends on the teachers' and parents' inability to tolerate a child's behaviors.

The United States Uses 90 Percent of the World's Ritalin

Desperate to do what was best for our child, we almost fell into the medication trap. We resisted, sensing that what the school called a problem was also our son's greatest strength. Since then we've learned that the United States manufactures and consumes about 90 percent of the Ritalin in the world, and that Virginia is among the top states relying on stimulant medication to control children.

Parents and teachers must try alternatives, and resist predicting a child's long-term future based on the behavior in first

The Percentage of Children Medicated for ADHD in the United States

This map shows the percentage by state of children four to seventeen years old (among those who have ever been diagnosed with ADHD) who have taken medication for the condition.

Legend:
- 5.5–6.5%
- 4.5–5.4%
- 3.5–4.4%
- 2.1–3.4%

States	Medicated	States	Medicated	States	Medicated
United States	4.3	Louisiana	6.3	Ohio	5.0
Alabama	6.5	Maine	4.5	Oklahoma	4.1
Alaska	4.0	Maryland	5.5	Oregon	3.8
Arizona	3.0	Massachusetts	5.4	Pennsylvania	5.3
Arkansas	6.5	Michigan	5.3	Rhode Island	5.9
California	2.1	Minnesota	4.7	South Carolina	6.2
Colorado	2.8	Mississippi	5.4	South Dakota	4.2
Connecticut	3.3	Missouri	4.5	Tennessee	4.8
Delaware	6.0	Montana	4.4	Texas	4.9
Florida	4.8	Nebraska	4.3	Utah	3.1
Georgia	5.6	Nevada	3.3	Vermont	3.8
Hawaii	2.7	New Hampshire	5.7	Virginia	5.5
Idaho	3.7	New Jersey	3.1	Washington	4.0
Illinois	3.3	New Mexico	3.5	Washington, DC	3.5
Indiana	5.0	New York	3.4	West Virginia	5.8
Iowa	5.5	North Carolina	6.1	Wisconsin	4.7
Kansas	5.3	North Dakota	4.4	Wyoming	4.0
Kentucky	4.8				

Taken from: Centers for Disease Control and Prevention, "State-Based Prevalence Data of ADHD Medication Treatment, National Survey of Children's Health, 2003. www.cdc.gov/mmwr/preview/mmwrhtml/mm5434a2.htm.

or second grade. Before thousands of other children go on medication, more long-term studies are needed about the behavior of young children and long-term success.

We've since become grateful for the struggle with Henrico's schools. Neighbors and co-workers were supportive. Henrico libraries and the First Unitarian Church of Richmond provided settings where Nick flourished.

ADHD Treatment Is Not Consistent

Other children are less fortunate. A 20-fold variation in ADD/ADHD treatment exists among communities, which demonstrates the range of tolerance for children's behavior. Virginia researcher Gretchen B. LeFever reports that preliminary studies show no association "between the rate of Ritalin use and education outcomes at the school district level." Medicating children for problem behavior is an extreme reaction to the ordinary challenges of raising a child.

The conflict with Henrico strengthened our family and made us focus on our behavior and goals. We care about one another. We value self-discipline and education. Our son realized that his parents had high expectations, believing in his potential regardless of others' opinions.

Parents and schools can never stop believing in any child's potential. Society should hold high expectations for every individual, never resorting too quickly to stereotypes that limit opportunities and dreams—particularly those of children.

FOUR

Many Children Who Could Benefit from ADHD Medication Do Not Receive It

Washington University School of Medicine

> This press release from the Washington University School of Medicine reveals the results of a scientific study regarding the use of medication in children with ADHD. According to the release, the results of the study contradict claims that children with ADHD are overmedicated. The study looked at 1,610 twins, evaluated them to determine who fully met the criteria for ADHD, and then looked at the medications they were taking. Results indicated that the percentage of children with ADHD who were not taking any ADHD medications was quite high, and the percentage of children who did not fully meet the criteria for ADHD but were taking ADHD medications was extremely low.

In contrast to claims that children are being overmedicated for attention-deficit/hyperactivity disorder (ADHD), a team of researchers at Washington University School of Medicine in St. Louis has found that a high percentage of kids with ADHD

Washington University School of Medicine, "Washington University Researchers Find Almost Half of Kids with ADHD Are Not Being Treated," August 4, 2006. Used with permission of Washington University School of Medicine.

are not receiving treatment. In fact, almost half of the children who might benefit from ADHD drugs were not getting them.

"What we found was somewhat surprising," says Richard D. Todd, M.D., Ph.D., the Blanche F. Ittleson Professor of Psychiatry and professor of genetics. "Only about 58 percent of boys and about 45 percent of girls who had a diagnosis of full-scale ADHD got any medication at all."

More Children Are Taking ADHD Drugs

Much has been written about the increasing number of children taking drugs for ADHD. One study found that the percentage of elementary school children taking medication for ADHD more than tripled, rising from 0.6 percent in 1975 to 3 percent by 1987. Another study reported that the number of adolescents taking ADHD drugs increased 2.5 fold between 1990 and 1995. And many reports have noted a rapid increase in the U.S. manufacture of the stimulant drug methylphenidate—usually sold under the brand names Ritalin or Concerta.

The researchers studied 1,610 twins between the ages of 7 and 17. Of those, 359 met full criteria for ADHD: 302 boys and 57 girls. The total number of boys in the sample was 1,006, and 604 girls were included

Many More Children Could Benefit from ADHD Drugs

"From a clinical point of view, this study affirms that for whatever reason, many children who could benefit from treatment are not receiving it," says first author Wendy Reich, Ph.D., research professor of psychiatry in the William Greenleaf Eliot Division of Child Psychiatry.

It's possible those children aren't being identified at schools or pediatrician's offices or that their parents are choosing not to put their children on stimulant medication, according to Reich.

"It may be that mental health professionals need to do a better job of explaining the risks and benefits of treatment," Todd says.

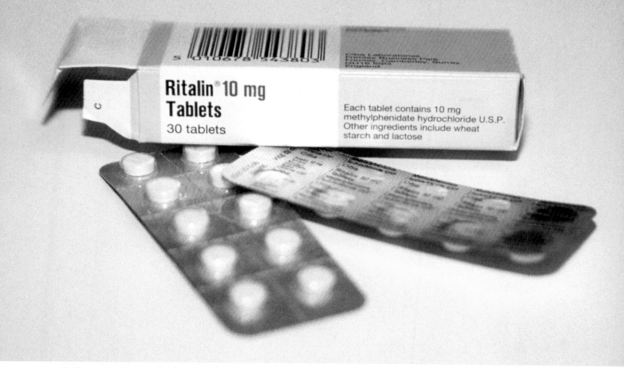

Many experts believe that children with ADHD are not getting the medications they need.

"The vast majority of parents whose children were involved in this study reported that their kids improved with medication, and when used properly these drugs have been shown to be very safe."

Some Children Without ADHD Take ADHD Medication

Todd, who also is the chief of child psychiatry, says among the 1,251 kids in the study who did not have ADHD, some did take stimulant medications, but it was a very small percentage, only 3.6 percent of the boys and 2.6 percent of the girls.

He says, however, that in many cases, there's an understandable reason those children have sought treatment. The study found that most of the children without ADHD who took medication did have some symptoms of ADHD—some hyperactivity or problems with inattention—but not enough symptoms to meet

Many Children and Teens with ADHD Do Not Seek or Receive Treatment

In one study, from a sample of 1,610 young people, 359 met the diagnostic criteria for ADHD. Of those 359, 266 had sought treatment for ADHD. Of those 266, 203 had received medication for ADHD.

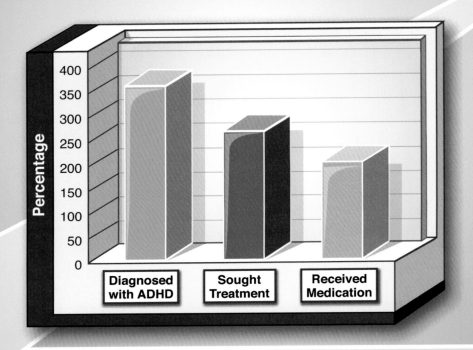

Taken from: Wendy Reich, Hongyan Huang, and Richard D. Todd, "ADHD Medication Use in a Population-Based Sample of Twins," *Journal of American Academy of Child and Adolescent Psychiatry*, vol. 45, no. 7, July 2006, pp. 801–807. Copyright 2006 Journal of the American Academy of Child and Adolescent Psychiatry.

formal diagnostic criteria as defined by the American Psychiatric Association's *Diagnostic Statistical Manual (DSM-IV)*. The study also found that most of the kids who took medication without an ADHD diagnosis had a twin who did have the disorder.

"These children have what we might call subsyndromal, or mild, forms of ADHD, and they seemed to come from families where other children had full-blown ADHD," Todd explains. "We didn't find that children got these drugs because they had other problems, such as conduct disorder or a learning disability."

Reich says the eventual goal of studying twins is to learn what elements of ADHD are passed down in families. She says some aspects of the disorder are certainly genetic. Others may be related to environmental factors, and studying twins allows the researchers to tease out those influences. Todd says the hope is to identify genes that contribute to the disorder, or rather, the disorders.

"It's becoming clearer that ADHD is not a single problem but a group of disorders that have different causes but similar clinical expressions," he explains. "There also can be lots of reasons why you become diabetic or hypertensive. The end result is high blood sugar or elevated blood pressure, but how that happens can differ greatly from individual to individual. It's the same thing for ADHD."

Fewer Girls Receive Treatment

Todd believes that as genes are identified, it may become possible to intervene in new ways—with psychotherapies, environmental interventions or medications that affect biological pathways that haven't yet been identified. But he says a potential stumbling block in the future, as now, will involve getting children into treatment.

"That's especially true for girls because for whatever reason, less than half of the girls who had ADHD in this sample ever received treatment," Todd says. "As genes are discovered and treatments developed, they won't be able to solve problems unless they are used."

FIVE

ADHD Drugs Do Not Help Children Long Term

Nancy Shute

> Nancy Shute writes the "On Parenting" blog at *U.S. News & World Report Online*. In this viewpoint she reports on a study published in the *Journal of the American Academy of Child and Adolescent Psychiatry*. The Multimodal Treatment Study of Children with ADHD (the MTA study), which has tracked hundreds of children for eight years, recently found that children who had continued to take ADHD medication had just as many ADHD symptoms as the children not taking ADHD medication. Shute also interviews William Pelham, one of the researchers in the MTA study, asking what parents should do in light of the new findings. Pelham argues that, although behavioral treatments may require more effort and more expense than medication, they can be very effective in addressing the symptoms of ADHD. Medications, he maintains, do not offer long-term benefits for children.

Stimulant drugs like Ritalin that are used to treat ADHD don't improve children's symptoms long term, according to new research published online in the *Journal of the American Academy of Child and Adolescent Psychiatry*. That may come as a surprise to parents, but ADHD researchers have been arguing for the past 10 years over the findings of the Multimodal Treatment Study of Children with ADHD. Called the MTA study, it is the largest study conducted to compare the benefits of medication to behavioral interventions.

This latest report from the MTA study tracked 485 children for eight years and found those still taking stimulant medication fared no better in the reduction of symptoms such as inattention and hyperactivity or in social functioning than those who hadn't. Most of the children who had taken medication for the first 14 months were no longer taking it. This, the researchers wrote, raises "questions about whether medication treatment beyond two years continues to be beneficial or needed at all." Earlier reports found that children taking stimulants alone or combined with behavioral treatment did better in the first year than children who got no special care or who got behavioral treatment alone.

There's more: Stimulant drugs stunt children's growth, according to another report in the journal that analyzes MTA data. Children who never took stimulants were three quarters of an inch taller and 6 pounds heavier on average than children who took medication for three years. The children don't make up for that later on.

What's a parent to do with this new information? To find out, I talked with William Pelham, a pioneer in the study of behavioral treatments for ADHD and one of many researchers who participated in the MTA study. Pelham is a distinguished professor of psychology at the University of Buffalo. Here's an edited version of our conversation:

Nancy Shute: You have long been critical of earlier interpretations of the MTA study, which said that stimulant drugs were better at relieving ADHD symptoms than behavioral treatment. Why is that?

William Pelham: The investigators in the study have not owned up to the fact that the results at one year were dramatically different than the results at all the follow-ups. The group has continued to state the usefulness of long-term treatment, when the data show very clearly that it did not help.

ADHD Symptoms After Thirty-Six Months of Different Treatments

In one study, children were randomly assigned to a specific treatment for ADHD. After three years all the groups demonstrated fewer ADHD symptoms, but none of the treatments seemed to be more effective than any of the others. Researchers theorize this may be due to symptoms decreasing over time or, for those assigned to treatment with medication, to children not consistently taking the medication prescribed.

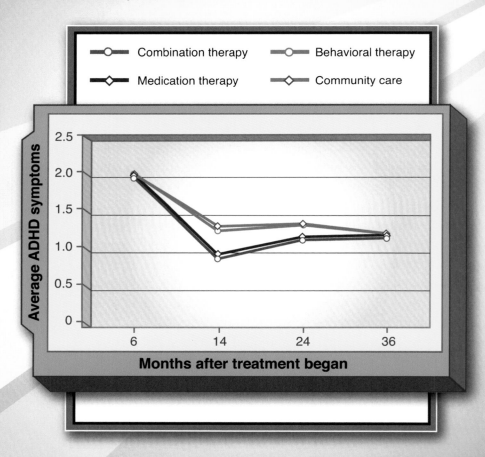

Taken from: Peter S. Jensen et al., "3-Year Follow-Up of the NIMH MTA Study," *Journal of the American Academy of Child and Adolescent Psychiatry*, vol. 46, no. 8, August 2007, p. 996. Copyright 2007 American Academy of Child and Adolescent Psychiatry.

If you put a child on medication, he or she is far better right at that time. The question for parents is: Is this going to make a benefit for my child long term? The answer is no. Behavioral treatments are going to have much better benefit in the long term. Unfortunately, we don't have studies of the long-term effects of behavioral therapies eight years out, because they're much harder to do. But theoretically, we know they work.

Shute: It's easy to find a doctor who will prescribe Ritalin. But many parents feel it's hard to find good behavioral interventions for ADHD.

Pelham: It's true that it's harder to find than medication. But it's not true that it can't be found. Behavioral parent training is widely available—it is not rocket science, and it's proven to help. School-based interventions for ADHD are also widely available. Almost every teacher in the country knows good behavior management techniques for children with ADHD. What's not as available are the intensive peer programs, which is what we do. We developed an intensive summer program that has the best supported evidence of any program. That's been replicated in a number of places, including New York University, the Cleveland Clinic, and the University of Alabama-Birmingham. It's not as widely available as it should be. But it's wrong for a doctor to say to a parent, this treatment is harder to find, so instead we're going to put your child on a drug that will have no long-term benefit.

Shute: Families often have a hard time paying for behavioral therapies. Is that true with ADHD?

Pelham: Many insurers do not include coverage for psychosocial treatments for ADHD in their plans. They won't pay for the types of interventions that are most evidence-based. That's a problem; that's a public health problem that people at the state and national level need to work on. If Blue Cross Blue Shield paid for behavioral parent training, I assure you it would be everywhere. It's also true for Medicaid. There are many states where Medicaid won't pay for this, even though it's the most solidly evidence-based treatment of all childhood behavioral disorders.

Because many insurers do not cover psychosocial therapy for ADHD, parents who cannot afford such treatment often seek medication for their child's condition.

Shute: The Institute of Medicine [IOM] just came out with a report saying that many of these behavioral interventions can actually prevent problems. Can you give me an example?

Pelham: There's the good behavior game, a very common classroom management tool [in which the class is rewarded for good behavior] that is used for kids with ADHD. If that was used around the country, not only would it be good prevention for behavioral problems generally, it would treat ADHD. We're using the Good Behavior Game in one of our studies.

Another example is the Positive Parenting Program, which is one of 10 really good evidence-based behavioral parent-training programs.

The IOM has not argued to put Ritalin in the water as a prevention. They're recommending taking the effective psychosocial things we know work and making them widely available. If that happened, there would be much less need to medicate ADHD kids.

SIX

ADHD Drugs Do Not Increase the Risk of Substance Abuse

Arline Kaplan

A link between substance abuse and prior use of prescription drugs for ADHD has been suggested by past scientific studies. The following selection by Arline Kaplan, a health writer for *Psychiatric Times*, reports on two newer studies that contradict this theory, however. The first study found that boys who started taking stimulants at a younger age were far less likely to abuse substances than boys beginning the prescriptions at an older age. The second study did not find such a difference based on the age of starting medications and also did not find that ADHD drugs increased the risk for substance abuse later in life.

Two recent studies present clinical evidence that the use of stimulants to treat boys with attention deficit hyperactivity disorder (ADHD) does not increase their risk of later substance use disorders. This evidence provides clinicians and families with much needed reassurance.

"It is very important for families to know that treatment does not increase the risk of substance abuse in late adolescence and early adulthood; this information should be a key source of comfort to them," said Joseph Biederman, MD, professor of psychiatry at Harvard Medical School and chief of pediatric psychopharmacology at Massachusetts General Hospital, both in Boston, and lead author of a naturalistic 10-year follow-up study on ADHD.

ADHD affects between 5% and 10% of children and adolescents. One of the great debates in childhood psychiatry has been whether widespread use of stimulants to treat ADHD might lead to later substance use disorder. The idea is theoretically plausible, according to researchers, because both stimulant medications and drugs of abuse increase concentrations of dopamine in the nucleus accumbens—the neural mechanism considered crucial for their reinforcing effects. Also, some studies have suggested a causal link between stimulant treatment in childhood and later substance use disorder.

That was not the case, however, in a 17-year prospective follow-up study conducted by Salvatore Mannuzza, PhD, and colleagues. Coauthor Francisco Castellanos, MD, professor of child and adolescent psychiatry at New York University and director of research for its Child Study Center, said that the study is one of the "most methodologically sound" of those that cumulatively suggest that medication treatment does not increase the long-term risk of substance abuse problems.

A Less Conservative Approach May Be Appropriate

Results of the Mannuzza study might influence clinical practice, Castellanos told *Psychiatric Times*. He explained that he and many other clinicians have adhered to a conservative approach and waited as long as possible before prescribing stimulants for a child with ADHD, "based on the general principle that the longer we can wait, the more brain development can occur unaffected by any medication. . . . Now, I would say we shouldn't try to hold out to the very last minute; there may really be a cost to doing that.

"The study looks at ADHD from childhood through the late 20s," Castellanos said. "We found no evidence that treatment with stimulants at younger ages had a deleterious effect. In fact . . . having medication treatment at earlier ages may have had a beneficial effect."

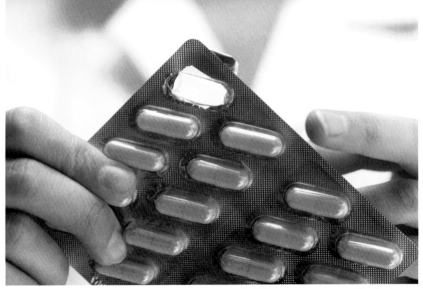

A report by researchers at New York University concluded that ADHD medication does not increase the long-term risk of substance abuse.

One Study Found Early Treatment Worked Best

The team conducted a prospective longitudinal study of 176 white, middle-class boys (aged 6 to 12) who were treated for ADHD with methylphenidate (Ritalin, Concerta, Metadate, Methylin). At baseline, none of the youngsters displayed conduct disorder, which is regarded as a precursor of antisocial personality disorder and a risk factor for substance abuse. The participants were followed through late adolescence and into adulthood. For comparison, the researchers also tracked 178 boys without ADHD.

Boys with ADHD who started stimulant treatment early (at age 6 or 7) faced a lower risk of later drug abuse than those who began taking the medication later (at ages 8 through 12), the team reported.

Among participants who were treated early, 27% abused drugs by their mid-20s—a percentage close to that of comparison participants without ADHD (29%). In contrast, substance use disorders developed in 44% of the boys who were treated later.

Researchers used 9 predictor variables, including the child's age at initiation of methylphenidate treatment, treatment duration, dosage, severity of hyperactivity, socioeconomic status, and life-time parental psychopathology. None of the predictor variables accounted for the association between age at treatment initiation and non-alcohol substance use disorder.

"Unexpectedly, the development of antisocial personality disorder accounted for the association between age at first treatment with methylphenidate and substance abuse," the researchers said. They added that "it is unclear why age at initiation of . . . treatment and . . . later development of substance use and antisocial personality disorder appear to be related."

Currently, the team is conducting an adult follow-up study on the participants, now in their 30s and 40s. MRI scans are being used.

"We will be able to see whether there are any measurable structural differences in their brains that might be related to their . . . diagnosis; how that diagnosis developed over time; whether they were affected by when they started treatment and how long they were in treatment; and whether any of that was related to how their lives turned out," Castellanos said.

A Second Study Indicates No Increased Risk of Addiction

The team led by Biederman assessed 112 young men 10 years after ADHD had been diagnosed. They ranged in age from 16 to 27 years at the time of their reassessment; 82 (73%) had been treated with stimulants at some time and 25 (22%) were currently receiving stimulant treatment.

"This was a naturalistic study and not a clinical trial," Biederman said, "so the children were using the medication as prescribed by their treating physicians for varied periods of time."

The mean age at stimulant treatment onset was 8.8 years. Half of the patients began treatment between 6 and 10 years of age. The mean duration of treatment was 6 years; 50% of patients underwent stimulant treatment for 2 to 10 years.

Study participants were interviewed using standard tools for assessment of psychiatric disorders. Additional questions were

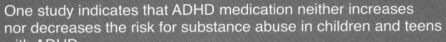

A Comparison of Substance Use Disorders Among Men Treated with and Not Treated with Stimulants for ADHD

One study indicates that ADHD medication neither increases nor decreases the risk for substance abuse in children and teens with ADHD once they become young adults.

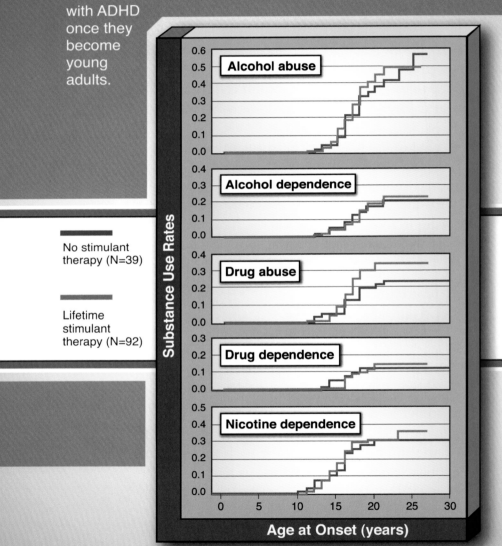

asked about their use of nicotine, alcohol, and various psychoactive drugs (such as cocaine, amphetamines, sedatives, opiates, and nonprescription sleeping or diet pills).

The follow-up study, which controlled for the presence of conduct disorder in the original diagnosis, found no evidence that "prior treatment with stimulants was associated with subsequent increased or decreased risk for alcohol, drug, or nicotine use disorders."

"Our work also documents that the use of stimulants does not hasten or increase the risk of substance abuse in those children who use [them] for a long time," Biederman said.

Early Treatment Made No Difference

In addition, no significant association was detected between the age at onset of stimulant treatment and subsequent substance use disorders. Those results differed from an earlier study by Biederman and colleagues. That 1999 report was a 4-year follow-up of adolescents in the same sample that detected a protective effect of stimulant treatment.

"There may be some protective effect by adolescence, but it is not maintained into adult life," Biederman said.

"We do not know why the protective effect of stimulants is not evident in adulthood," said Biederman and colleagues. "It is possible that because of parental monitoring, treatment compliance—and hence efficacy—is greater for youths than adults. Another possibility is that because adolescents have not fully passed through the age of risk [for] substance use disorders, stimulants may delay rather than stop subsequent substance use disorders."

Noting limitations with their 10-year follow-up study, Biederman and colleagues warned that their results may not be the same in children with ADHD in the general population, especially in females and in those of other racial or ethnic backgrounds. However, information on females is forthcoming. Biederman told *Psychiatric Times* that his team has just completed a study on females with ADHD and submitted it for publication.

"We found results similar to those in boys," he said.

ADHD and Substance Use Disorder

While the studies by Biederman and colleagues and Mannuzza and associates showed that stimulant treatment for ADHD does not increase the risk of substance abuse in adulthood, both research teams acknowledged that childhood ADHD itself is significantly associated with adolescent and adult substance use disorders.

In an editorial in the May 2008 issue of the *American Journal of Psychiatry*, Nora Volkow, MD, director of the National Institute on Drug Abuse, and James Swanson, PhD, the University of California at Irvine, said that the studies "highlight the need to develop a better understanding of the natural history of ADHD over time," and also the "need for the development of integrated treatments that target both ADHD and substance abuse in order to go beyond standard treatment and find a way to reduce or prevent substance abuse and provide better treatments if these disabling outcomes emerge."

Substance abuse prevention is an important and very challenging area, Castellanos said. "We know that nicotine is usually the gateway drug, and kids are starting to use nicotine in middle school. Often it is the impulsive, hyperactive kids who are among the leaders in that process, so . . . having parents know what is going on, talking to each other, and being extremely firm about [avoiding] nicotine in all of its forms—that's a battle . . . parents want to be fighting."

SEVEN

The FDA Should Investigate ADHD Drugs More Quickly and Thoroughly

Chuck Grassley

> Chuck Grassley, a Republican senator from Iowa since 1981, is a member of the U.S. Senate Committee on Finance. In the following letter from Grassley to Andrew C. Von Eschenbach, the commissioner of the U.S. Food and Drug Administration (FDA), Grassley notes the dramatic increase of sales of ADHD drugs in the United States as well as the adverse-event reports for these drugs. He focuses on three ADHD drugs—Adderall XR, Concerta, and Strattera—and the safety concerns that have been raised regarding them. He urges the FDA to speed up its investigations of these drugs.

The United States Senate Committee on Finance (Committee) has exclusive jurisdiction over the Medicare and Medicaid programs, and, accordingly, a responsibility to the more than 80 million Americans who receive health care coverage under these programs. Each year Medicare and Medicaid pay hundreds of millions of dollars for prescription drugs, including reimbursement for prescription drugs used to treat Attention

Chuck Grassley, "Grassley Questions FDA's Approach to Managing Attention Deficit Prescription Drugs," letter to U.S. Food and Drug Administration. http://finance.senate.gov/press/Gpress/2005/prg020706.pdf.

Deficit and Hyperactivity Disorder (ADHD). As Chairman of the Committee, I write out of concern regarding the Food and Drug Administration's (FDA) handling of the safety concerns associated with the class of drugs indicated for treatment of ADHD, including Adderall, Concerta, and Strattera, and whether or not the drugs' long-term risks have been adequately and promptly explored.

The Use of ADHD Drugs Has Increased

Sales of ADHD drugs have skyrocketed over the past few years. IMS Health reports that ADHD drugs sales increased over threefold between 2000 and 2004, from a total of $759 million

Senator Chuck Grassley (R-IA), pictured, argues that the Food and Drug Administration needs to investigate further the long-term safety of taking such drugs as Adderall XR, Concerta, and Strattera—all of which are used to treat ADHD.

to $3.1 billion. Whether or not ADHD drugs are overprescribed to children remains extremely controversial. Yet, in this context of increased ADHD drug treatment, it does not appear that FDA has taken a comprehensive approach toward addressing the potential cardiovascular and psychiatric risks associated with this class of drugs. Rather, FDA's actions appear ad hoc and disjointed, leaving serious questions in the minds of the parents of 2.5 million children and adolescents who use ADHD medications.

This past year, adverse event reports for these ADHD drugs have detailed cardiovascular episodes, such as hypertension, chest pain, arrhythmias and tachycardia (rapid heartbeat), among others. Additionally, concerns were raised regarding sudden unexplained deaths (SUD), strokes, and various psychiatric events—including reports of abnormal behavior, aggression, anxiety, depression, and suicidal thoughts. Each of these adverse events presents serious and possibly life threatening side effects for those using these prescription drugs to treat ADHD.

Adderall XR

In February 2005, cardiovascular concerns raised in adverse event reports ultimately led Health Canada (the Canadian equivalent of FDA) to suspend market authorization of Adderall XR for six months. Health Canada's temporary suspension of Adderall XR was based upon post-marketing reports compiled in the United States. According to Health Canada, the decision came as "a result of a thorough review of safety information provided by the manufacturer, which indicated there were 20 international reports of sudden death."

At the same time that Canada decided to suspend use of Adderall XR, FDA "[did] not believe that any immediate changes [were] warranted in FDA's labeling or approved use of the drug." However, FDA did note that it had required the modification of the labeling for Adderall XR in August of 2004 to include a warning to patients with an underlying heart defect that they might be at an increased risk for sudden death.

Concerta

Last summer, the safety of ADHD drugs was again called into question when FDA publicly stated that it had concerns about possible psychiatric side effects stemming from the use of Concerta for the treatment of ADHD. Specifically, FDA stated on its website that it had "identified two possible safety concerns with the methylphenidate drug products: psychiatric adverse events and cardiovascular adverse events." These statements were made in conjunction with the June 29 and 30, 2005 meeting of FDA's Pediatric Advisory Committee.

Over the course of the two-day meeting, the Pediatric Advisory Committee discussed the cardiovascular and psychiatric adverse events reported to FDA. Through spirited discussion the various members of the Pediatric Advisory Committee expressed concerns that label changes to methylphenidate products may be necessary for both cardiovascular and psychiatric side effects. Ultimately, the Pediatric Advisory Committee decided that moving too quickly with label changes could alarm the public and according to press accounts, would hold off making any recommendations regarding the Concerta label until an FDA review of the entire class of drugs could be completed in early 2006.

Strattera

In September of 2005, FDA issued an alert to Healthcare Professionals regarding the use of Strattera in children and adolescents. The public health advisory directed Eli Lilly, the manufacturer of Strattera, to "revise the labeling . . . to include a boxed warning and additional warning statements regarding an increased risk of suicidal thinking in children and adolescents." FDA cited data showing an increase in suicidal thoughts among those in 12 separate studies, including one individual who attempted suicide.

Upcoming Advisory Committee Meetings

FDA recently announced meetings of two different advisory committees to examine adverse events related to ADHD drugs. In

From 2004 to 2008, prescriptions for ADHD drugs have increased every year.

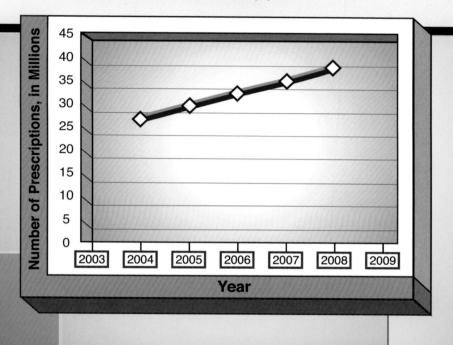

Taken from: Keith Simmons, "Our View on Helping Hyperactive Kids," *USA Today*, April 13, 2009.

early January 2006, the FDA announced a meeting of the Drug Safety and Risk Management Advisory Committee (DSaRM), which is scheduled for February 9–10, 2006. According to the DSaRM agenda, "[c]ases of sudden death and serious adverse events including hypertension, myocardial infarction, and stroke have been reported to the [FDA] in association with therapeutic doses of drugs used to treat Attention Deficit Hyperactivity Disorder (ADHD) in both pediatric and adult populations."

On the first day of the DSaRM meeting, "the committee will be asked to discuss approaches that could be used to study whether these products increase the risk of adverse cardiovascular outcomes." On the second day of the DSaRM meeting, "the committee will be briefed on agency actions for the COX-2 selective Nonsteroidal Anti-Inflammatory Drugs (NSAIDs)," among other issues. . . .

Two weeks ago [January 2006], the FDA announced another meeting to examine adverse events of ADHD drugs before the Pediatric Advisory Committee. FDA stated that it would convene the Pediatric Advisory Committee on March 22, 2006, to discuss neuropsychiatric adverse events associated with ADHD medications for the pediatric population. In the announcement, FDA stated that this panel will also "receive an update on efforts to better understand cardiovascular adverse events."

Comprehensive Review Is Needed

While I am pleased that FDA has convened both the DSaRM advisory panel to discuss cardiovascular concerns and the Pediatric Advisory Committee to discuss neuropsychiatric adverse events, I remain concerned that lost between the two meetings is a comprehensive review of all adverse events for this entire class of medication for all populations served. It is understandable that FDA would use multiple panels to review some of the ADHD drugs individually, mainly because there are so many drugs used to treat ADHD. However, at some point a comprehensive review of the entire class of ADHD drugs would be beneficial to the millions of Americans taking ADHD medications and the parents of the 2.5 million children on these drugs.

Further, I remain concerned that while both psychiatric and cardiovascular risk signals have cropped up across this class of drugs this past year, it appears that FDA is just now beginning to "discuss approaches" for studying these risks. More specifically, I question why it has taken nearly an entire year for FDA to begin to address these concerns given the serious nature of the adverse events associated with these drugs.

EIGHT

The FDA Is Appropriately Examining the Safety of ADHD Drugs

U.S. Food and Drug Administration

> The following selection is a communication from the U.S. Food and Drug Administration (FDA) responding to a study published in the *American Journal of Psychiatry* that examined the safety of drugs prescribed to children with ADHD. The FDA and the National Institute of Mental Health (NIMH) paid for the research. The study examined the likelihood that a child's sudden death was caused by ADHD medication and concluded that there may be a link between the two. The FDA, however, points out weaknesses in the study and does not advise that parents should stop giving their children the medication as prescribed.

The U.S. Food and Drug Administration is providing its perspective on data published today [June 23, 2009] in the *American Journal of Psychiatry* on the potential risks of stimulant medications used to treat Attention-Deficit/Hyperactivity Disorder (ADHD) in children.

U.S. Food and Drug Administration, "Communication About an Ongoing Safety Review of Stimulant Medications Used in Children with Attention-Deficit/Hyperactivity Disorder (ADHD)," June 23, 2009. www.fda.gov/Drugs/DrugSafety/PostmarketDrugSafetyInformationfor PatientsandProviders/DrugSafetyInformationforHeathcareProfessionals/ucm165858.htm.

Given the limitations of this study's methodology, the FDA is unable to conclude that these data affect the overall risk and benefit profile of stimulant medications used to treat ADHD in children.

Therefore, the FDA believes that this study should not serve as a basis for parents to stop a child's stimulant medication. Parents should discuss concerns about the use of these medicines with the prescribing healthcare professional. The FDA's summary of the study and its limitations, and our recommendations for healthcare professionals, are provided below.

Study Summary

This study, funded by the FDA and the National Institute of Mental Health (NIMH), compared the use of stimulant medications in 564 healthy children from across the United States who died suddenly to the use of stimulant medications in 564 children who died as passengers in a motor vehicle accident. Use of stimulant medication was determined from parents, medical examiners, and toxicology reports. These two groups of children were compared because the children all died suddenly and the cause of death was not a known health problem.

The Findings of the Study

- Out of 564 healthy children who died suddenly, 10 were reported to be taking a stimulant medication at the time of death.
- Out of 564 healthy children who died in a motor vehicle accident, 2 were reported to be taking a stimulant medication at the time of death.
- The study authors concluded that there may be an association between the use of stimulant medications and sudden death in healthy children.

The Limitations of the Study Data

- A child's use of a stimulant medication for ADHD was determined many years after each child's death. The deaths

Cases of Sudden Death Reported to the FDA Advisory Committee

Patients	Amphetamines		Methylphenidate	
	Unadjudicated sudden deaths	Cases meeting WHO criteria for sudden death	Unadjudicated sudden deaths	Cases meeting WHO criteria for sudden death
Age, 1–18 years		12		7
Age, >18 years		5		1
Total	28	17	16	8

Data are from the Adverse Event Reporting System of the Food and Drug Administration (FDA). Amphetamines include mixed amphetamine salts (Adderall), amphetamine, biphetamine, and dextroamphetamin. *WHO* denotes the World Health Organization. Unadjudicated sudden deaths are cases that have not been settled by a legal proceeding.

Taken from: Steven E. Nissen, "ADHD Drugs and Cardiovascular Risk," *New England Journal of Medicine*, vol. 354, no. 14, April 6, 2006.

occurred between 1985 to 1996, but the data on medication usage were collected from March 1997 to January 2008. This time lag may have resulted in reporting errors.

• The differences in cause of death (sudden death versus death from a motor vehicle accident) could have influenced the family or caregiver's recall of information on stimulant medication use at the time of death, creating an elevated rate of stimulant drug use in the group of children who died suddenly, as compared to the children who died in a motor vehicle accident.

- The sudden unexplained death of a child, in comparison to a death of a child from a motor vehicle accident, may have increased the likelihood of a post-mortem inquiry into medication use.
- The low frequency of stimulant use in both groups, as well as possible differences in the type of post-mortem inquiry, could have a profound biasing effect on the results.

Ongoing FDA Review

The FDA is continuing its review of the strengths and limitations of this and other epidemiological studies that evaluate the risks of stimulant medications used to treat ADHD in children. The Agency for Healthcare Research and Quality (AHRQ) and the FDA are sponsoring a large epidemiological study that will

Staff members of the Food and Drug Administration listen to a presentation on a study of a drug used to treat ADHD.

provide further information about the potential risks associated with stimulant medication use in children. The data collection for this study will be complete later in 2009.

Recommendations for Health-Care Professionals

Follow all the current prescribing information for use of these medications, including:

- Take a medical history for cardiovascular disease in the child and his or her family.
- Perform a physical exam with special focus on the cardio-vascular system (including examination for the signs of Marfan syndrome [a genetic disorder of the connective tissue]).
- Consider obtaining further tests such as a screening electrocardiogram and echocardiogram if the history or examination suggests underlying risk for or the presence of heart disease.

The FDA intends to update this advisory when additional information or analyses become available.

Adverse reactions or quality problems experienced with the use of this Product may be reported to the FDA's MedWatch Adverse Event Reporting program either online, by regular mail or by fax. . . .

Any child who develops cardiovascular symptoms (such as chest pain, shortness of breath or fainting) during stimulant medication treatment should immediately be seen by a doctor.

Prescription stimulant medications are indicated for the treatment of ADHD as part of a comprehensive treatment plan. ADHD is a persistent pattern of inattention and/or hyperactivity-impulsivity that is more severe than expected for a child's developmental age. Although estimates vary, ADHD is diagnosed in about 4% to 10% of children in the United States (more boys than girls). Children with untreated ADHD may have significantly higher rates of behavioral, mood and anxiety disorders, often resulting in problems with family, school and friends.

NINE

Advertising Has Increased ADHD Drug Use

Karin Klein

> The use of certain ADHD medications dramatically increased from 2001 to 2005. In this viewpoint Karin Klein, an editorial writer for the *Los Angeles Times*, points out that this increase coincides with magazine advertising campaigns for the same drugs. She also explains that despite a United Nations Treaty banning the marketing of this class of medication, drug companies have been allowed to continue to advertise and that the United States, the only country to ignore the ban, has by far the highest consumption of ADHD drugs. Klein concludes by calling on the Federal Drug Administration to enforce the ban.

Back-to-school season is in full swing. Time to pick out a backpack, sneakers and a stimulant for attention-deficit hyperactivity disorder.

Nearly 2 million children in the United States are diagnosed with ADHD, which is marked by poor concentration, lack of self-control and/or hyperactivity. Besides time off from school, many kids with ADHD get a summer "vacation" from the prescription medications that help them focus in class.

So August has become a prime time to market the idea that a change in drug for the new school year (Concerta to Adderall?)

Karin Klein, "Pencils, Pens, Meds," *Los Angeles Times*, August 20, 2007. Reproduced by permission.

might help the kids focus better, keep them going longer or have fewer side effects. Direct-to-parent marketing of ADHD drugs—most of which are stimulants—has grown pervasive over the last few years, despite a United Nations treaty banning most of it. Use of such medications increased by more than 60% from 2001 to 2005, according to the International Narcotics Control Board.

The Percentage of Children Ever Diagnosed with ADHD, 2003

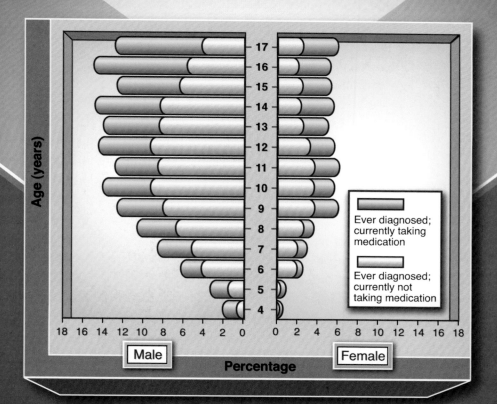

Taken from: *MMWR Weekly*, "Mental Health in the United States: Prevalence of Diagnosis and Medication Treatment for Attention Deficit Hyperactivity Disorder—United States, 2003," September 2, 2005. www.cdc.gov/mmwr/preview/mmwrhtml/mm5434a2.htm.

This month's homemaker-targeted magazines, such as *Family Circle*, *Woman's Day* and *Redbook*, feature advertising spreads for Vyvanse, Shire US Inc.'s new entry in the growing stable of ADHD medications. The ads show "Consistent Kevin through the day, even through homework," picturing a well-groomed boy smiling as he wields his pencil through a work sheet, and "Consistent Sarah," who even at 6 P.M. contentedly pecks away at the piano keys.

ADDitude magazine, published for people with ADHD, has ads for four medications. One ad touts a flavored, chewable form of methylphenidate with the slogan, "Give me the grape." (Methylphenidate is best known under the trade name Ritalin, which is not among those drugs advertised.)

An Advertising Ban

Ads for candy-flavored methylphenidate are a far cry from the vision set forth in 1971 by the Convention on Psychotropic Substances. So far, 159 countries, including the U.S., have agreed to ban consumer-targeted marketing of psychotropic medications—which all these ADHD drugs are—that carry the potential for addiction or dependency. For decades, pharmaceutical companies abided by its provisions.

But in 2001, one company began buying ads in the September issue of women's magazines in the U.S. to draw attention to Metadate CD, a long-acting form of methylphenidate. Other companies quickly followed suit.

Called on the carpet by the U.S. Drug Enforcement Administration, lawyers for the drug companies vowed to defend themselves under the umbrella of 1st Amendment speech rights. According to former DEA officials, the Department of Justice was unwilling to test this one in court.

Increased Use of ADHD Drugs

Six years later, the results are dramatic. Doctors and therapists increasingly see parents seeking to change their child's medication or coming in with their own diagnosis of ADHD and suggestions for medications they have seen advertised. Many of the companies offer coupons for a free trial supply.

Children in the U.S. are 10 times more likely to take a stimulant medication for ADHD than are kids in Europe. In fairness, children in Europe are also somewhat less likely to be diagnosed with ADHD because of a stricter set of criteria. But that doesn't nearly account for the difference in prescription rates. The U.S., the only nation to violate the U.N. treaty, consumes about 85% of the stimulants manufactured for ADHD.

Following heavy advertising by drug companies, the use of ADHD medications such as Adderall increased by 60 percent from 2001 to 2005.

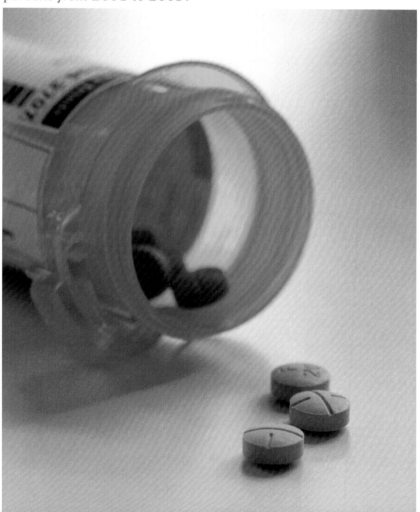

Though the drugs do not appear to be habit-forming in children with ADHD, there's a rising black market for methylphenidate and similar drugs. A report last year by the National Institute on Drug Abuse found that teenage abuse of prescription stimulants was rising.

A Correlation in Consumption

Drug companies would argue that increased production and use of ADHD drugs are the result of better diagnosis and treatment. But the International Narcotics Control Board holds advertising responsible. In a report earlier this year, the board noted that from 2001—when the ads first appeared—to 2005, medical consumption of methylphenidate increased by 64%.

"That large increase was mainly a result of developments in the United States, where the substance is advertised in the media, directly to potential customers," according to the report.

The Food and Drug Administration should move forward with rules to bring the U.S. into compliance—in conjunction with the Justice Department. There's legitimate debate about Americans' rush to diagnose and medicate children who fall problematically outside the norm. In some cases, the drugs are the only thing that keeps a child from being expelled for aggressive behavior, or falling into the foster-care system, or believing that he is an impossibly bad or stupid kid. Yet other countries are making do with far less of the medications.

Powerful psychotropic medications should be an option of last resort and uninfluenced deliberation, not another brand-name product to add to the back-to-school shopping list.

TEN

ADHD Drugs Are Misused by Students

Harry Jaffe and Alex Chip

> Adderall is a common medication prescribed for ADHD. However, high school and college students not diagnosed with ADHD are using it to help them study and do well on tests and also as a party drug. In this viewpoint Harry Jaffe, a national editor for the *Washingtonian*, and Alex Chip, a former *Washingtonian* editorial intern and recent Duke University graduate, write about Adderall use by students. Profiles of several students and an interview with a Drug Enforcement Administration (DEA) pharmacologist explore the dangers of Adderall and shed light on how students use the drug to help them succeed in school.

Pressure began to mount for Lisa the night before she was to take the SAT exam. Curled up beneath her gold comforter, she flipped the channels on her TV and thought, "What if I fail?"

Lisa knew she had everything a 17-year-old could want: a loving family, a nice boyfriend, good grades, a bright future. Her blond hair and brown eyes made her popular with the boys. She volunteered with kindergartners; she ran cross-country. Her mother described her as "a good, hard-working kid with a great heart."

"But none of these things matter if I flunk the SAT and don't get into a good college," Lisa worried. She knew the first thing

Harry Jaffe and Alex Chip, "ADD & Abusing Adderall," Washingtonian.com, vol. 41, January 2006, pp. 41–47. Reproduced by permission.

many people in Washington [D.C.] ask is "Where did you go to school?"

Lisa's alarm broke her troubled sleep at 7:30, 90 minutes before she had to be at Walt Whitman High. She drank a glass of orange juice and gathered her number-two pencils, calculator, and school ID.

Walking into Whitman, Lisa ignored her friends' chatter. She tried to focus on advice from the College Board Web site: Answer easy questions first, guess smart, don't panic.

"Don't panic?" she thought.

Proctors distributed tests, the room grew quiet, Lisa tried to concentrate. A half hour into the test, she "zoned out." Long before the proctor announced the end of the sixth section, she put down her pencil and closed the test booklet. She did not open it for the final verbal section.

Back at home, she called her boyfriend.

"How did you do?" he asked.

"I gave up halfway through," she said.

A New Strategy

Three months later, as her boyfriend negotiated the traffic to DC's Wilson High School, where she would take the test again, Lisa prepared for the SAT a different way—with a cup of coffee, a croissant from 7-Eleven, and a 30-milligram Adderall pill.

Adderall is an amphetamine that doctors prescribe to help people with attention deficit hyperactivity disorder. Lisa didn't have the disorder or a prescription. She got the pills—sometimes blue, sometimes pale orange, depending on dosage—from friends.

Stepping through the metal detector at Wilson High, Lisa felt a rush of euphoria and confidence. She tore into the opening page, furiously scribbling equations and inequalities in the margin of her test booklet.

When she emerged from the building after the exam, she was still factoring quadratic equations from the test on her scratch paper. She slipped into her boyfriend's car.

"So you didn't quit on this one?" he asked.

"I could take that thing three more times today," she said.

The first time Lisa took the SAT, she scored 950. This time, with Adderall, she improved to 1050. Her father, a college professor, wasn't satisfied. She took an SAT class, dropped another 30-milligram dose of Adderall, and scored 1150.

Now she's a freshman at George Washington [GW] University —thanks, she believes, to Adderall.

A Common Experience

Adderall is "the drug in the drawer" for many high-school and college students. "Everyone seems to have it," says Emily Schwartz, a GW freshman.

Mary Katherine Stump, a Georgetown University student, wrote in a column in a school newspaper: "During finals week here at Georgetown, campus turns into an Adderall drug den.

The widespread use of Adderall by college students, both to study and to party, has risen in recent years.

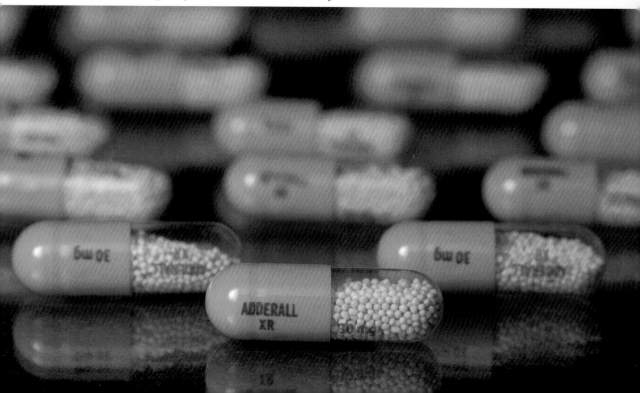

Everyone from a cappella singers to newspaper writers become addicts, while anyone with a prescription and an understanding of the free market becomes an instant pusherman."

In the 1960s, the Rolling Stones dubbed tranquilizers and antidepressants "mother's little helper." Forty years later, Adderall is "brother's little helper." And sister's.

Prescribed liberally by psychiatrists to young people who they believe have a learning disability, such as ADHD, Adderall is easier to get on some campuses than a can of beer. Students who do not get it by prescription beg or buy a few pills from friends. Some students take Adderall to sharpen their focus; some crush and snort it to get a high.

"It seems to be quite ubiquitous on the college-campus level," says Gretchen Feussner, a pharmacologist with the Drug Enforcement Administration [DEA]. Under federal laws, she says, Adderall is a Schedule II stimulant; selling or distributing the drug is a federal crime. But it is seldom enforced.

What Is Adderall?

Adderall is a chemical compound of amphetamine and dextroamphetamine. It comes in four main strengths: 5, 10, 20, and 30 milligrams. Warnings with the medication say it has a high potential for abuse. Says the Web site Rx List, "Administration of amphetamines for prolonged periods of time may lead to drug dependence and must be avoided."

Among Adderall's side effects are elevated blood pressure, restlessness, dizziness, insomnia, euphoria, dryness of mouth, diarrhea, constipation, and impotence.

In street terms, Adderall is "speed" in a very low dose. Methamphetamine, the drug made in clandestine labs that is tearing up families and communities across the country, is speed in high doses.

"Adderall is the primary amphetamine on the market now," says Feussner. According to IMS America, which studies drug use, 11 million prescriptions were written for amphetamine products in the U.S. in 2004; more than 7 million were for Adderall.

In treating attention-deficit disorders and hyperactivity, Adderall is an alternative to Ritalin and other drugs such as Concerta and Strattera. Most have similar effects. For patients who suffer from hyperactivity, Adderall has a calming effect. But "average" people who have no problem focusing or staying calm often find that Adderall sharpens their focus.

"Everyone's attention span is improved by taking low doses of a stimulant," says Feussner.

There are no hard statistics on how many college students use Adderall. A University of Wisconsin study put the number at 20 percent. Our informal survey at colleges in this region suggests that some 25 percent of students have used Adderall at least once to study or to party.

A Sign of the Times

In a society that encourages people to take pills for everything from sleeplessness to erectile dysfunction, popping an Adderall now and then doesn't seem shocking. Have federal agencies studied its use and abuse? Says Jules Asher, a spokesman for the National Institute of Mental Health [NIMH], "Adderall is one of the things that gets kicked around between DEA, NIMH, and NIDA [National Institute on Drug Abuse]. It seems to have fallen through the cracks."

Canadian health authorities pulled Adderall from shelves last February [2005]. Health Canada [the Canadian equivalent of FDA] cited results from a study by Shire Pharmaceuticals, Adderall's manufacturer, that reported 20 sudden deaths worldwide. The FDA reviewed the study, determined that the deaths were caused by preexisting heart problems, and required Shire to add a warning to its pills. Canada has since lifted its ban.

Is there a downside to taking the drug? Should Adderall taken for a boost in test scores be regulated like steroids used by athletes to boost physical strength?

"There are side effects and toxicity when Adderall is taken in an unregulated way," says David Zwerdling, a Silver Spring [Maryland] psychiatrist. He knows Adderall is being diverted and says he and pharmacists are taking more care in dispensing it. He implores parents to keep control of the pills.

"In college that breaks down," he says. "Who's going to control this medication?"

A Dangerous Drug

Kirk entered the Bryan Research Center at Duke University and hurried to Room 103 for his 10 AM class—Pharmacology 160: Drugs, Brain, and Behavior.

"Good morning," Cynthia Kuhn said to the 40 students. She turned to the blackboard and wrote ADDERALL. "I realize," she said, "that many of you may be using a friend's Adderall for studying or recreational purposes, not comprehending the danger, but the truth is that snorting Adderall can be worse for you than snorting cocaine."

She went on to describe the dangers of snorting nonprescribed Adderall, which increases its potency and likelihood of adverse side effects.

Kirk squirmed in his seat. "I didn't know that," he said to Claire, the brunette sitting next to him. But Kirk knew that Adderall was more dangerous than his friends at Duke were willing to admit.

Tall and lanky with olive skin and brown eyes, Kirk grew up in western Loudoun County, about 40 miles from DC. His parents came here from India. He was considered the pride of the family. He wants to go to medical school at George Washington University and fulfill his parents' dream of having their eldest son become a doctor.

Kirk worked hard to get into Duke but found he had to work much harder to compete with the other premed students. He barely kept up his grades his freshman year.

First semester sophomore year, Kirk started to sample Duke's party scene, which didn't help his grades, especially in organic chemistry. Nor did skipping class half the time. The evening before the first exam, Kirk was studying and sweating in the library. A fraternity brother picked up on his distress.

"Want to try an Adderall?" he asked. "It will help."

Nonmedical Use of Adderall, 2005–2006

This graph shows the percentage of college students and others aged eighteen to twenty-two who reported using Adderall for nonmedical purposes in the year prior to 2006–2007.

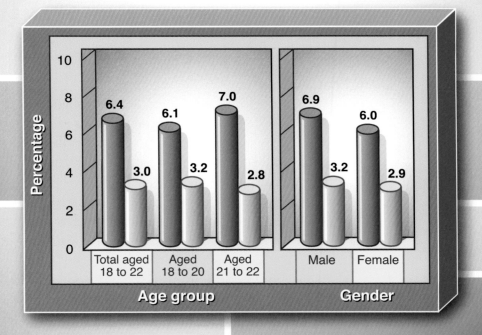

Taken from: Substance Abuse and Mental Health Services Administration, National Surveys on Drug Use and Health, 2006–2007. http://oas.samhsa.gov/sk9/adderall/adderall.pdf.

Motivated by Panic

Kirk had never taken a pill for work or play. He'd never smoked pot. But his anxiety about taking drugs was overwhelmed by the thought of a D in chemistry on his medical-school applications. "Sure," he said.

He swallowed a 20-milligram tablet in the library at about 10 PM. The test was at 2 the next afternoon. He studied for 14 straight hours. He aced the exam.

Adderall became a staple in Kirk's academic routine: skip class and homework for weeks, take an Adderall to cram before the test. It didn't bother Kirk that he would crash afterward. He would sleep through the rest of the day and wake up "feeling as if a tiny midget had been kicking and punching me while I slept."

At first Kirk's life was improved by Adderall. The same drug that led him to dance on tables at 4 A.M. also kept him on the dean's list despite his class absences.

Dangerous Results

One Tuesday night before winter break, Kirk crushed more than 40 milligrams of Adderall. He had knocked off a physics exam that afternoon. He was determined to drink all night. He snorted the Adderall and reached into the refrigerator for a beer. His legs buckled, and he passed out.

Kirk awoke in the morning in a pool of vomit with the worst hangover of his life. He swore off Adderall as a recreational stimulant. He figured if he limited the drug to schoolwork, he could control it.

Final exams exert enormous pressure at schools like Duke. Kirk braved the December winds night after night to hole up in the library. Over five days he took 200 milligrams of Adderall and slept a total of ten hours.

On the morning of his fourth and final test, Kirk's heart began to beat quickly, and a fever burned his face. His roommate rushed him to the hospital with a temperature of 103.5 degrees.

Kirk missed the final exam for his Behavior/Neuroscience class and had to get a dean's excuse to take it after winter break. With the cold compresses on his forehead and chest, the stern skepticism of the dean, and the worry in his parents' faces, it wasn't an experience he wanted to repeat.

Kirk was remembering that experience as Professor Kuhn described how Adderall affects brain chemistry, by boosting dopamine and serotonin, and increases heart rate. Claire tapped his knee.

"I don't care what Dr. Kuhn says—I'm still going to use Adderall, at least for the MCAT," she said. "What about you?"

Kirk considered the question and realized that Claire, like most students, would never admit that Adderall was dangerous. And though he hadn't touched it since his hospitalization four months earlier, he couldn't imagine taking an eight-hour test like the MCAT without it. He looked at Claire and whispered, "Sure am."

The DEA's Viewpoint

Gretchen Feussner, the DEA pharmacologist, is not surprised that premed students would drop some Adderall before taking an admissions test.

"We know Adderall is used by college students for a variety of reasons," she says, "primarily to study."

We are sitting in an "intel" conference room at DEA head-quarters in Pentagon City. This is where DEA agents track shipments of cocaine from Colombia and heroin from Afghanistan. Digital clocks track time from here to Kabul. Flat-screen TV monitors hang on the walls. But Adderall isn't on the DEA's radar.

"We don't see that many problems with Adderall," says Feussner, who has been reviewing prescription drugs for 15 years. "We don't have any idea how many kids are abusing this substance."

She says: "If you take Adderall, you face the same dangers as taking cocaine and meth. Your tolerance goes up; you can get addicted. But there's no data showing that it's happening."

In comparison to methamphetamine—speed made in clandestine labs by the likes of motorcycle gangs—the DEA sees Adderall as a middle- and upper-class designer drug.

"Adderall has the same potential for abuse as meth or cocaine but it is not viewed as a serious drug of abuse," Feussner says.

But because Adderall is a Schedule II stimulant, distributing it without a prescription is a violation of federal law.

"Yes," she says, "it's against the law. But who's going to pick up on that? DEA agents are not invited onto college campuses. We are not there to be Mom and Dad. We don't target campuses. They are not our mission."

A Societal Issue

Feussner has downgraded Adderall to a societal issue. "We give kids the message that if they take this or that medication, things will be better," she says. "Have a three-martini lunch? Take an Adderall and get focused. Trouble sleeping? Take a Xanax."

Is Adderall a no-fault drug?

"If the use is continued and the dose escalates," she says, "they're setting themselves up for a real problem, especially if there's a history of addiction in the family. It could escalate to cocaine.

"It's important for us to give the message that kids should stay away from this drug without telling horror stories," she adds. "We don't want to lie to them. It's a delicate balance of how much information to give. They might say, 'Gee, I want some.'" . . .

Facing the Downside

Adderall is not for everyone. Take Andrew. The University of Maryland junior started college with a heavy load of math courses for his engineering major. "I was taking a Calculus II course and hadn't gone to class or studied," he says. "I had to learn a whole course in six hours."

Adderall was "always around" his dorm. Half the kids on his hall were regular users. He bought two white pills from a girl down the hall for $5, dropped both, studied for six hours, and did well on the exam.

"Next day my brain was hurting," he says. "I passed out."

Nevertheless, Andrew kept taking Adderall on occasion to study. One day in his sophomore year he took a stronger dose to study for an engineering exam. It took an hour to kick in.

"When I got up to take a drink of water, I didn't feel right," he says. "I sat back down and still felt unsteady. I focused for another two hours and tried to go to sleep. My heart was pounding. No way I could sleep."

He went to a movie and passed out.

"After that I didn't use Adderall," he says. "I realized it wasn't a good idea to wait until the last minute to study. I manage my time better.

"My grades have improved," he says. "I guess I grew out of it."

Success Without Adderall

Rebecca Dreilinger returned to Brandeis University after Thanksgiving break in 2004 daunted by her workload. She had to finish her senior thesis on Spanish-language media coverage of the U.S. 2004 presidential campaign. "I was stumped," she says.

Dreilinger was working out in the school gym and talking to a friend about her problems writing the thesis. Another student overheard them and walked over.

"I heard you talking about your paper," she said. "Have you thought of trying Adderall? You'll never write a better paper."

Dreilinger grew up in Bethesda [Maryland] and graduated from Holton-Arms, a top private school for girls. Competitive as Holton was, the pressures there were light compared to expectations at Brandeis. Dreilinger was working hard and getting good grades; she wanted to keep it that way.

She remembered her cousin talking at Thanksgiving about students using Adderall at the University of Virginia. "At the library, everyone is totally cracked out on Adderall," her cousin had said. "It's not fair. Why should they be able to party, take a pill, come to the library all bleary-eyed, cram, and get good grades?"

In the gym at Brandeis, Dreilinger thanked the student who offered the Adderall but declined. She went back to her dorm and worked on her thesis. But she was stuck. She could not organize her research into a coherent paper.

At her computer, she was about to e-mail the girl from the gym and take her up on her Adderall. The phone rang. It was her mother. They didn't discuss the paper or the pill.

"Just hearing from her was enough," says Dreilinger. "I knew she would kill me if she knew I had taken a drug to get me through."

Dreilinger bore down and finished the thesis on her own.

"It was a tough paper to write," she says, "but it would be mine, good or bad. If I had used Adderall, I never really would have known what I'm capable of doing on my own."

An Unfair Advantage?

While Rebecca and Andrew turned away from Adderall, clearly many students use it regularly for the boost they get, in either grades or pleasure.

But the questions remain: How dangerous is it? Is it ethical? Does it give students an unfair advantage over others who don't use it? Or is it just par for the course in today's pharmaceutical world?

"It's using chemistry to help yourself through problems," says Beth Kane Davidson, director of the Addiction Treatment Center at Suburban Hospital. "It is what we do as a society. That's why our treatment centers are full."

ELEVEN

Behavior Therapy Is a Good Alternative to ADHD Medication

Laura Flynn McCarthy

Writing for *ADDitute*, a magazine for people with an interest in ADHD, Laura Flynn McCarthy explores the role of behavior therapy for children with ADHD. Drawing on interviews with physicians and psychologists, McCarthy explains what behavior therapy is, its benefits, and how it works. Many doctors recommend behavior therapy for all children with ADHD because it gives children coping skills and self-confidence, and, for those taking medication, it may enable them to take a lower dose. Early intervention may even prevent ADHD from developing in children genetically prone to the disorder. McCarthy cautions, however, that for behavior therapy to work, parents, children, and teachers must all take part in the training.

I magine a treatment that could manage the behavior of a child with attention deficit disorder (ADD), make you a better parent, and enlist teachers to help him do well in school—all without the side effects of ADHD medications.

There *is* such a treatment. It's called behavior therapy—a series of techniques to improve parenting skills and a child's behavior.

"When I first diagnose a child with ADHD, I tell the parents they need to learn behavior techniques, whether I'm prescribing medication or not," says Patricia Quinn, M.D., co-author of *Understanding Women with AD/HD* and *When Moms and Kids Have ADD*, and who has treated ADD patients in Washington, D.C., for more than 25 years.

"A pill decreases common ADHD symptoms like impulsivity and distractibility, but it doesn't change behavior. A child on medication might be disinclined to punch someone, because he's less impulsive, but he doesn't know what to do instead. Behavior therapy fills in the blanks, by giving a child positive alternative behaviors to use."

Quinn is not alone in prescribing behavior therapy for patients. According to the American Psychological Association, it should be the first line of treatment for children with ADHD who are under five years of age.

William Pelham, Ph.D., director of the Center for Children and Families at the State University of New York, goes further, suggesting that children of any age try it before medication.

Behavior Therapy Works

"There's clear evidence that a behavioral approach will work for the majority of children with ADHD," says Pelham. "The benefit of using behavior therapy first is that, if a child also needs medication, he can often get by with a smaller dose."

Recent evidence suggests that children who are put on medication first never try behavior therapy—or they try it years later, if medication has stopped working. According to a four-year study Pelham is conducting on medication and behavior therapy, at the University at Buffalo, "Parents who see that medication is working are less motivated to follow through with behavior therapy. That would be fine if the data showed that medication alone helped the long-term trajectory of ADHD kids. It doesn't."

According to Pelham, a child can take medication for 10 years, and the day you take him off of it—or he decides not to take it any more, as some 90 percent of teenagers do—the benefits stop. Then what? "It's a lot harder to learn from scratch how to deal with a teenager who's acting out than it is with a five-year-old who is acting out," he says. "The parent has lost five or 10 years relying on medication and not dealing with problems that behavior therapy could have addressed."

What Pelham doesn't point out is that successfully implementing behavior therapy at home is hard work. It requires that you and your child change the way you interact with each other—and that you maintain those changes over time. Unlike the benefits of medication, behavioral improvements may not be apparent for weeks or months.

"The benefits a child receives from behavioral treatment are strongly influenced by the ability of the parent to consistently implement the program plan," says Thomas E. Brown, Ph.D., assistant clinical professor of psychiatry at Yale University School of Medicine.

The Earlier, the Better

Although it's never too late for a child to benefit from behavior therapy, evidence suggests that it works best when started early in the child's life. Younger children generally have simpler problems, and these may be responsive to behavior therapy. For younger children, parent-child interactions aren't ingrained and may be easier to change.

"Studies show that the average ADHD child has one to two negative interactions per minute with parents, peers, and teachers," says Pelham. "If you extrapolate, that's half a million negative interactions a year. Either you sit back and let your child have those negative experiences, or you intervene early and do something to stop them."

Quinn suggests that the longer a parent interacts negatively with her child, the greater the chances he will develop secondary behaviors, like oppositional defiant disorder, anxiety and/or depression, and low self-esteem. "You can avoid such problems by treating early with behavior therapy."

Some studies show that the earlier a child receives ADHD behavior therapy, the better chance he or she has of coping with ADHD later in life.

Behavior Therapy May Prevent ADHD

An intriguing new study suggests that using behavior therapy early in a child's life may actually prevent ADHD or minimize its severity. Neuroscientists at the University of Oregon studied children ages 18 to 21 months old who had a gene called the "7 repeat allele," which has been associated with ADHD. This gene is present in about 25 percent of children who have the condition.

The researchers observed the children's behavior and their interactions with parents. They found that children whose parents scored highest in measures of "parent effectiveness" (gauged by how supportive they were and how well they interacted with their kids) were less likely to show symptoms of ADHD than children with the gene whose parents scored lower.

"It appears that, in children who have a genetic susceptibility to ADHD, things can be done to prevent it," says Michael I. Posner, Ph.D., professor emeritus of psychology at the University of Oregon, who headed the study. "Good parenting may be part of that."

"Although, in some cases, ADHD is inevitable, in a high percentage of children, ADHD occurs because of environmental influences, including the kinds of interactions they have with their parents early in life," says James Swanson, Ph.D., professor of pediatrics at the University of California in Irvine.

Quinn disagrees. "Swanson seems to be saying that parents are the cause of ADHD," she says. "Yet it's been established that ADHD is a genetic or inherited disorder in a majority of cases. It is true that parents can make the condition worse or better. Employing appropriate parenting techniques is something they can do to make it better, and to modify the impact that ADHD behaviors have on the child and the family."

How It Works

Behavior therapy operates on a simple premise: Parents and other adults in a child's life set clear expectations for their child's behavior. They praise and reward positive behavior and discourage negative behavior.

"All behavior therapy programs should include four principles," says Swanson:

1) Reinforce good behavior with a reward system—stars on a chart or extending a special privilege, like playing a favorite video game for an extra half-hour or going to a movie on Friday night.

2) Discourage negative behavior by ignoring it—according to experts, a child often uses bad behavior to get attention.

3) Take away a privilege if the negative behavior is too serious to ignore.

4) Remove common triggers of bad behavior.

If a child often misbehaves when sitting next to a particular buddy in the classroom, ask the teacher to re-assign your child to another seat.

"Behavior therapy isn't a cure-all for ADHD behaviors," says Quinn. "Parents who think they can change a long laundry list of behaviors will be disappointed." Pick five or fewer that you deem the most important.

The most effective programs include parent training, teacher/classroom strategies, and social-skills training for children. Many are based on the COPE [Community Parent Education] program, whose goal is to strengthen the parent-child relationship by teaching strategies in a group setting. Here is the [three-part] program that Pelham uses with good results:

Parent Training

Goal: To learn strategies to encourage positive behavior in your child and strengthen your relationship with him.

How long: Eight to 12 weekly sessions, lasting one to two hours, with fellow parents and a counselor/therapist.

Format: A group of parents views a film of a parent and child confronting a common problem, such as a child's tantrum in the grocery store. The group discusses better ways to handle it than by yelling at the child or threatening him.

One example: Parents state their expectations to the child before going into the store: "I'm going to shop for 15 minutes, and I expect you to walk beside me and help me look for things. If you whine, yell, or complain, we'll go out and wait in the car until you settle down, and then we will go back into the store. If you cooperate, then we will finish shopping quickly and have time to play in the yard when we get home." The counselor and parents practice the strategy on each other, and parents are

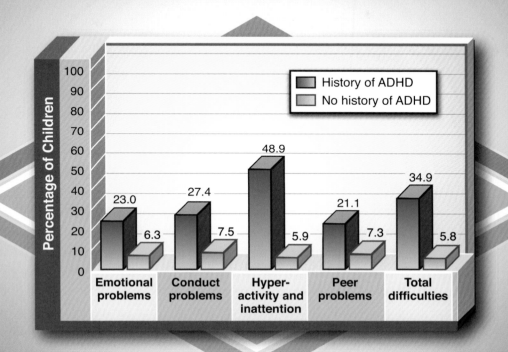

Problems Among Teens and Children Aged Four to Seventeen with and Without ADHD

Legend:
- History of ADHD
- No history of ADHD

Category	History of ADHD	No history of ADHD
Emotional problems	23.0	6.3
Conduct problems	27.4	7.5
Hyperactivity and inattention	48.9	5.9
Peer problems	21.1	7.3
Total difficulties	34.9	5.8

Y-axis: Percentage of Children (0 to 100)

Taken from: Tara W. Strine et al., "Emotional and Behavioral Difficulties and Impairments in Everyday Functioning Among Children with a History of Attention-Deficit/Hyperactivity Disorder," *Preventing Chronic Disease*, vol. 3, no. 2, April 2006, p.4. www.cdc.gov/pcd/issues/2006/apr/05_0171.htm.

asked to use it at home in as many situations as they can. At the next session, parents discuss the strategy's success, view another film, and learn the next strategy.

Skills learned: To establish house rules and structure (posting chore lists and morning and evening routines); to praise appropriate behaviors and ignore mildly inappropriate ones; to use commands ("Sit down, please") and not questions ("Why won't you sit down?") and to be specific ("You need to sit in the chair and not wiggle while I tie your shoelaces"); to use when-then contingencies ("When you finish your homework, then you can ride your bike"); to establish ground rules, rewards, and consequences before an activity; to use timeouts effectively (giving a child one minute of timeout for each year of age); to create daily charts and point/token systems to reward good behavior.

Child Training

Goal: To help children acquire the social skills needed to form lasting friendships. Research shows that kids with ADHD who learn to make friends do much better in life than those who don't.

How long: Peer groups meet weekly in after-school or weekend sessions, for two to three hours, throughout the year. Another option is summer day camp, led by a therapist. The program runs six to eight weeks, six to nine hours a day.

Format: Sessions begin with a brief discussion of a social skill or a common peer issue, and the counselor offers strategies for mastering the skill or dealing with the problem. Then kids play games—soccer, basketball, board games—and the counselor looks for opportunities to praise them for positive interactions, good social skills, and sportsmanship. For example, during a basketball game, the counselor may compliment a child for passing the ball to his teammates.

Skills learned: To problem-solve (a child may role-play different ways to cope when someone calls him a name); to become more competent at games and sports, which can help a child fit in better socially; to decrease undesirable and antisocial behaviors, like bossiness and aggression.

Teacher Training

Goal: To help teachers adapt the goals of the parent-training program to the classroom.

How long: From one hour to one day to a weekend of training at the school or at an off-site seminar.

Format: This varies, depending on the school and the professional you're working with. In many cases, the behavior therapist will agree to speak with the school psychologist and teacher about addressing the needs of your child. If not, you will have to set up an appointment to talk with them. "Perhaps the best approach," says Pelham, "is developing a 504 Plan[1] that allows you to establish behavior goals for your child. And it won't cost you anything."

Skills learned: To develop class rules and goals, using small rewards to encourage compliance (rewards are written on poster board and hung up in the classroom); to give positive reinforcement and specific instruction at a child's desk ("Today, you are just reading about animals and picking one you would like to write about; you don't have to write anything during this class period"); to use when-then contingencies ("When you finish your required assignment, then you can have some free time to play a game"); to use a daily report card to communicate with parents.

Program Particulars

"This three-part program is effective because it is so intensive," says Quinn. "However, it's tough to find this kind of program in many communities—and if you do, it is very expensive." . . . Full-blown programs, like Pelham's, cost $5,000 to $6,000 a year, while summer treatment camps for children run from $2,000 to $4,000. Parent training with a therapist can cost $10 to $100 per session.

Most insurance plans cover 20 sessions a year with a therapist, according to Pelham, but generally won't pay for summer camp or social skills training. Some do, however, so consult your plan's administrator.

More Affordable Alternatives

If you don't have the time or money for an intensive program, there are less ambitious options. Check with your community mental health center or mental health hospital to see if they run

1. A 504 plan, referring to Section 504 of the Rehabilitation Act and the Americans with Disabilities Act, details the modifications and accommodations that will be made for students with special needs.

behavior programs. According to Pelham, "Community mental health centers are required to document that they are using so-called 'evidence-based' programs, like parent training, in order to receive federal funding. If they're not offering it, ask the health center, 'Why not?'"

No matter which program you use, look to include classroom strategies. "The teacher must be included and on the same page, or the therapy won't be effective," says Quinn. "You can't change a child's behavior only at night and on weekends. You have to do it all day long."

While experts point to behavior therapy's ability to change a child's behavior at school and at home, Quinn says there are longer-lasting benefits—self-control and empowerment. "You don't want a child with ADHD thinking he can act right only if he takes his meds," she says. "He needs to feel that he is responsible for getting good grades, he is smart, he is taking the initiative to make his bed. Behavior therapy does that. It gives a child control of his life." Every parent would consider that a great return on their investment.

TWELVE

Diet Can Help Treat ADHD

Carlotta Mast

With autism and ADHD affecting millions of children, some parents and practitioners are looking at diet as a factor. In an article for *Delicious Living*, a magazine focusing on natural foods and health-care methods, Carlotta Mast interviews medical practitioners and parents who attribute improvements in children's behavior to a change in diet. Mast explains that a gluten- and casein-free (GFCF) diet and a diet rich in magnesium and zinc may help children with autism and ADHD. Although success is currently anecdotal, research is under way that is investigating the claims.

Watching his 5-year-old son participate in a holiday pageant at school last December, Gary Greaves says he was blown away by how much Brandon had changed since first being diagnosed with autism in 2005. "We thought he would have to go to a school for autistic children," says Greaves, "but Brandon has improved enough that he is able to be in a normal kindergarten class. We wouldn't have dreamed of that a year and a half ago."

Greaves and his wife tried various treatments for their son, but eliminating dairy, gluten, and soy from Brandon's diet packed the greatest therapeutic punch, the Florida-based father

Carlotta Mast, "The Nutrition Link," *Delicious Living*, vol. 24, May 2008, pp. 30–35.
http://deliciouslivingmag.com. Reproduced by permission.

says. "Once we removed those, Brandon was a lot more verbal, and his tantrums were limited. He still has autism, but he is doing much better."

Behavioral and educational therapies continue to serve on the front lines of autism treatment. But mounting evidence shows that nutritional changes, including the removal of common problem foods, can benefit many autistic children, as well as those with other conditions that affect behavior and learning, such as attention deficit hyperactivity disorder (ADHD). "Many parents have come to realize that diet is an important piece [of the treatment puzzle for these children]," says Dana Laake, RDH, MS, LDN, and co-author of *The Kid-Friendly ADHD and Autism Cookbook* (Fair Winds, 2006).

Diet and the New Childhood Epidemics

Brandon Greaves is one of the estimated 1.5 million people in the U.S. living with autism, a complex condition that affects the normal functioning of the brain and inhibits social interactions and communication skills. ADHD—which is characterized by impulsiveness, hyperactivity, and the inability to focus—is another neurological disorder on the rise in young children, affecting an estimated 3 percent to 5 percent of U.S. school-aged kids.

Theories abound on why autism and ADHD cases have jumped dramatically, says Wendy Weber, ND, MPH, PhD, research associate professor at Bastyr University in Kenmore, Washington, Researchers continue to speculate about abnormalities in brain development; diets stripped of essential fatty acids, magnesium, and other crucial nutrients; and increased toxin exposure, which can be particularly detrimental to those children who are genetically built with an impaired ability to detoxify their systems. Researchers don't believe diet alone causes these conditions. But a growing number of physicians and families are adding diet interventions to their treatment plans because evidence shows that many children with autism and ADHD have problems digesting and absorbing nutrients from food, Laake says.

The Gut-Brain Connection

The gut-brain connection in autism and ADHD isn't yet fully understood, Weber says. However an increasing number of experts believe that many children with these conditions have food sensitivities and are unable to digest the proteins such as casein and gluten in specific foods. Signs of food sensitivity include gastrointestinal problems, chronic congestion, frequent ear infections, or cravings for specific problem foods, says Laake. Lab tests can help identify some sensitivities.

"I'd like to exchange these cola can tokens for a book on hyperactivity" cartoon by John Byrne. www.CartoonStock.com.

Casein (a protein found in dairy products), gluten (a plant protein found in wheat, rye, and other grains), and soy trigger the most problems, Laake says. Many researchers believe that when these foods are not completely digested, residue remains in the digestive tract in the form of peptides—short chains of amino acids. If the intestinal lining becomes too permeable or "leaky"—as is the case, theoretically, in many autistic and ADHD kids—these peptides get absorbed into the bloodstream, creating a morphine-like effect that can affect neurological functions, such as speech and auditory processing, and cause a child to zone out or withdraw from others, says Laake.

In some kids, food sensitivities produce symptoms that mimic signs of ADHD, including hyperactivity and the inability to focus. When kids eliminate trigger foods, their symptoms decrease substantially. "If we can identify and address food sensitivities, it can make a dramatic difference for some children," Weber says. "The challenge is figuring out which sensitivities they have."

The GFCF Diet

For Brandon Greaves, a gluten- and casein-free (GFCF) diet improved his gastrointestinal and behavioral symptoms and even led to increased language and social function. Nixing soy—another common problem food—helped, too. Kenneth Bock, MD, a family practice doctor in Rhinebeck, New York, and author of *Healing the New Childhood Epidemics* (Ballantine, 2007), says that although no dietary treatment works for every child, he cuts out gluten and casein for nearly all of his ADHD and autistic patients, for at least a period of time. The GFCF diet "turns lives around," Bock says. But, despite rising popularity among parents and doctors, the GFCF diet remains controversial.

Current anecdotal evidence suggests that elimination diets may help a surprising number of these kids. "Two-thirds of autistic children and around half of children with ADHD will benefit from a gluten- and casein-free diet," Laake says. But other experts say better research on the subject is needed. The few studies published to date each had design flaws and results contradict one another. Stay tuned, however: The results from a randomized, double-blind, placebo-controlled study sponsored by the National Institute of Mental Health are expected out this year [2008].

Laake advises an "elimination and challenge" approach, where one food is removed at a time and the child is monitored for symptoms. If no improvement is seen within one month, the food is reintroduced. "The best test is the child's own body," Laake says. Because gluten and casein are among the most common intolerances, Laake recommends eliminating foods that contain these first, followed by soy, corn, yeast, and other commonly reactive foods, if necessary.

Solving Nutrient Deficiencies

Fixing nutrient deficiencies can also have positive effects for kids with autism or ADHD. Because of their inability to properly digest food and absorb nutrients, many children with these disorders may be low in zinc, magnesium, B vitamins, iron, essential fatty acids, and other nutrients. These deficiencies, Laake says, can affect everything from behavior to what a carrot tastes like. She advises working with a nutritionist or other knowledgeable health care provider to run tests to pinpoint the exact nutrients lacking in a child's diet and devise a food and supplement program aimed at filling in the gaps.

Lack of magnesium, for instance, can cause hyperactive-like behavior, sound sensitivity, and irritability. Zinc deficiency—a result of a defect in zinc metabolism that's common in autistic children and can be exacerbated by diets high in white flour and other high-glycemic foods—can change a child's sense of taste and smell. This helps explain why autistic children are notoriously picky eaters, often willing to eat only macaroni and cheese, yogurt, and other bland food, Laake says. "For these children, many foods have either no taste or a foul taste." Poor taste perception won't improve until zinc levels rise. Feeding zinc-rich foods such as seafood, whole grains, beans, and cashews can

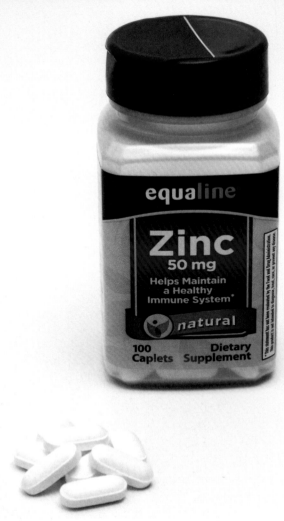

For ADHD sufferers, foods such as seafoods and whole grains provide needed zinc in their diets, but some may need to supplement their diet with zinc tablets.

help, but diet may not be sufficient to meet all of the child's zinc needs. Supplementation is usually the quickest way to get zinc into picky eaters, Laake says. . . .

Because autistic and ADHD kids are often very finicky eaters, Weber says improving and diversifying their diets may help. For her patients, she focuses first on protein-rich breakfasts, replacing foods made with refined flour and sugar with whole grains and fruits and vegetables, and serving water in place of soda or juice. By making these diet changes, Weber says, kids get crucial nutrients and balance their blood sugar levels—which is especially important for those prone to hyperactivity, inattentiveness, and mood swings.

Although Brandon Greaves' father admits that the diet changes aimed at helping a child with autism or ADHD aren't always easy to implement, he says such changes can actually benefit the entire family. "None of us eats fast food anymore," Greaves says. "It takes a little more time and effort, but we're all eating and feeling better."

THIRTEEN

Many Alternatives to Drugs Can Help Treat ADHD

Dawn McMullan

Looking for an effective treatment for her overactive child, Dawn McMullan turned to hemispheric integration therapy rather than medication or other alternatives. In the following viewpoint, which appeared in *D Magazine*, a publication that focuses on the Dallas/Fort Worth, Texas, area, McMullan explains the activities prescribed by a psychologist to rewire the brains of children with ADHD, autism and other disorders. She also discusses behavior modification therapy as an alternative to medications. The practitioners she interviews admit that there is little research to prove the effectiveness of alternative therapies, but they maintain that this is because most research on these disorders is funded by pharmaceutical companies and therefore the focus is on treatment with medication.

I don't remember a time when my 9-year-old son's body, mouth, or brain weren't in constant motion. Sometimes all three at once. Noah's tics have included licking things, twirling his hair until it started to fall out, chewing his hair, darting his eyes. He daydreams at school and can become belligerent after watching TV or playing games on the computer. Although not formally diagnosed, Noah is considered to be on the ADHD spectrum, meaning his ADHD (attention deficit hyperactivity disorder) isn't severe enough to be a huge problem for him scholastically or socially, but it is enough to make me occasionally want to tie him to a chair.

All that energy, though, is also part of who Noah is. There is no box big enough to contain his imagination and curiosity. While watching the sheepdog show at the State Fair last year, he asked how we knew the dogs were trained and not the sheep. This kind of thinking is why kids with the related problem, ADD (attention deficit disorder) can grow up to be ADD adults such as, it is now thought, Albert Einstein, F. Scott Fitzgerald, Robert Frost, and, more recently, Steven Spielberg.

So we've worked hard to find a treatment that works for Noah—something other than a pill. Twenty minutes wearing glasses with red-tinted lenses each day. Standing on his right leg for 60 seconds. Holding his body in a bridge form, one leg straight out, for 60 seconds. Repeat with other leg. One hour a day, three days a week, clapping along with a cowbell piped into headphones. Smelling a rotten onion five times a day with just his right nostril.

It's a regimen based on research into how the brain works. ADD and ADHD—the most common childhood psychiatric disorders—are all about how the brain is wired. And that wiring, some specialists insist, can be changed with targeted stimulation by simple exercises and tasks. It's a new way to treat the disorders, an approach that in some respects is a backlash to a time when the first and only option would have been a pill.

Ten years ago, ADD and ADHD medications were all the rage. Between 1990 and 1995, office visits for ADHD more than doubled. For that same time period, prescriptions for drugs such as Ritalin tripled for kids between the ages of 5 and 18. The most common drugs prescribed are Ritalin, Dexedrine, Cylert, and Adderall. Now, many parents are questioning their effectiveness, searching out other treatment options—hemispheric integration therapy (what we're doing with Noah), behavior modification, neurofeedback, biofeedback, sensory integration therapy, and occupational therapy.

A New Awareness

"There's more awareness of the complexity of the problem and the fact that there are other treatments," says Dr. Harvey Oshman, a Dallas clinical psychologist who is ADHD himself and a founder of ADD Associates. "I haven't seen a complete pendulum [away from medication], but you have a more sophisticated population. ADD is a very complex disorder. Sometimes we make it too simple."

When Vicki Brooks brought her then 7-year-old son Jonathan to Dr. David Clark's office, he was on his second ADHD medication as well as medication for depression. Clark, an East Dallas chiropractor trained as a chiropractic neurologist, did two things:

Some ADHD sufferers looking for alternative treatments may try aromatherapy.

noticed Jonathan's heart rate was 189 (twice what it should be) and changed the diagnosis to Asperger Syndrome, which is on the autism spectrum.

Clark placed Jonathan on a therapy schedule including daily exercises such as throwing a ball back and forth with his mom and catching it only with his left hand. The idea was to stimulate the right side of his brain, which wasn't functioning as well as his left. Jonathan also listened to music to stimulate the right brain. One day, he forgot to take his medication. His heart rate was normal. Off medication and with therapy, Jonathan's meltdowns in school stopped. His anxiety lessened. Now, he's a normal teenager who actually gets in trouble sometimes for goofing off, something unthinkable previously.

Behavior Modification Therapy

One of the better-known advocates of behavioral therapy for the treatment of these brain disorders is Wynford Dore, a U.K. [United Kingdom] native who founded a chain of clinics based on research spurred by the suicide attempt of his daughter Susie, who suffered from severe dyslexia. What was known when Dore organized his research team in 1999 was that in dyslexics (he hadn't yet gotten into ADD/ADHD), the cerebellum part of the brain was underdeveloped. Research with targeted exercises and tasks allowed Dore's team to measure cerebellum function as it generally caught up with the rest of the brain over the course of a year.

There are now 33 DORE Achievement Centers across the world, including a clinic in Grapevine [Texas], where Joe Stephens is DORE's co-chair and regional director of the southern United States. He says a recent study supports the success of behavioral therapy. Assessing 895 participants, of which about 73 percent had ADHD symptoms, the study showed that only 19 percent exhibited the symptoms after a year of treatment. "In the six years we've been doing this in the U.K., the patients don't come back," Stephens says. "There is no material regression."

In Clark's work with my son Noah, the scope of the therapy gets more specific. Clark, who says Noah is on the ADHD spectrum, wants to know what parts of the brain need help. Unlike DORE, which uses sophisticated equipment that was developed based on similar technology used by NASA to plot graphs of brain activity and eye movement, Clark employs a multistriped piece of cloth and the follow-my-finger game. He thinks Noah has issues with his orbitofrontal cortex and dorsolateral prefrontal cortex and their connections with an area known as the basal ganglia. Noah's red lenses, left leg balancing exercises, and time with the Interactive Metronome (the cowbell sound) stimulate the specific areas of his brain that need development.

Medication Can Be Helpful

For another patient, 11-year-old Daniel, the results are not yet clear. He sees the psychologist Oshman for behavior modification therapy but recently started seeing Clark, too. While skeptical of some of the behavioral approaches, Daniel's parents, Gail and Wayne, are willing to try. But they haven't given up on medication. When Daniel first started medication, it helped tremendously. "It took less than an hour," Gail says. "I could say to him, 'Put these socks in the dirty clothes', and he could walk from here to the dirty clothes and not be distracted by 500 other things he wanted to do."

Wayne has been treated for depression for years before his ADD diagnosis and is also seeing Oshman. Wayne says that since he started medication, his memory is better, he's more motivated, and he's able to follow through on projects. "I've always kind of felt like I never quite lived up to my potential," he says. "With the medication, it's like I can steer now in my life. I just feel like I can keep up with a list and I can knock things out. It's like the difference between feeling like you're coming off the day or you're on a roll and just starting. I'm just on track."

Lack of Research

Oshman doesn't at all discount alternative behavioral treatments, nor homeopathic remedies, nutritional changes, biofeedback, or

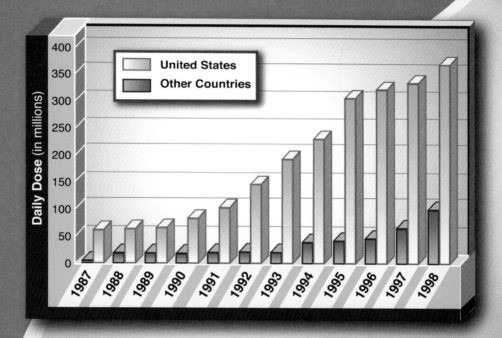

Consumption of the ADHD Drug Methylphenidate

The United States consumes more methylphenidate, the vast majority of which is prescribed for children with ADHD, than all other countries in the world combined.

Daily Dose (in millions)

- United States
- Other Countries

400
350
300
250
200
150
100
50
0

1987 1988 1989 1990 1991 1992 1993 1994 1995 1996 1997 1998

Taken from: Terrance Woodworth, Office of Diversion Control, Drug Enforcement Administration, Testimony Before Congressional Committee on Education and the Workforce, Subcommittee on Early Childhood, Youth, and Families, May 16, 2000.

neurofeedback. He says the problem with these treatments is a lack of formal research, not necessarily a lack of results. The main reason is money.

"There's not a great database of research to give support to those things," Oshman says, "One needs to understand drug companies are the ones who fund a lot of the research."

That helps explain why treatment of ADD/ADHD has, thus far, leaned to pharmaceutical approaches. "The pill is a very seductive and useful treatment," Oshman says. "It's a very good start. I don't want to dismiss it. But it's also extremely easy and needs to be combined with other treatments."

That's why it's important for parents to consider all the options. "There is such a huge gap in people who were willing to work with those kids and such a huge need for different treatment plans," Clark says. "People need to realize there are parts of the brain that are responsible for allowing your child to maintain focus, not be distracted, not be compulsive, not be impulsive"

More than Coping

With the right treatment, by stimulating and retraining targeted parts of the brain, Clark has seen patients with ADD, dyslexia, and autism do more than just live with their problems—they've overcome them. "There are so many people who have learned to cope because that's all they could do," Stephens says. "But they live a life that's less than their potential. The whole picture of the treatment paradigm has got to change."

There's nothing easy about this "other treatment" road. Several years into it, I can tell you that it's long, expensive, and time-consuming. Would it be easier to give my son a pill every morning than nag him about balancing exercises and cowbells? Sure. If his ADHD were more severe, would I medicate him? Maybe. Like everything else about parenting, there is no quick fix.

FOURTEEN

People with ADHD Can Have Successful Careers

Jan Farrington

Children and teens with ADHD often have trouble in school, and they and their parents may wonder how the disorder will affect their future. Writing for *Career World,* a magazine for students in middle and high school, Jan Farrington explains that people with ADHD can be extremely successful at what they do if they follow their interests and find work that fits their personalities. She shares the perspectives of people with ADHD who have interesting careers and how they found jobs that are right for them. Farrington also offers advice for people with ADHD for planning a career and for succeeding on the job.

In grade school, Rob Surratt was the kid who wiggled, squirmed, and "kicked the legs of the desk. I always needed to move around." Today Surratt, 21, a communications major (and part-time surfer) at the University of Hawaii, knows one thing for sure: "I don't plan to get a job where I sit in a cubicle all day."

Surratt, like an estimated 5 percent or more of Americans, has attention deficit disorder (ADD), a condition that makes it hard for people to concentrate, sit still, get organized, or finish the tasks they start.

High school was a tough time for Surratt, but over the years—with help from parents, teachers, and an ADD coach—

he has learned "what works" to help him stay focused and organized at school.

Now he's starting to think about his career. Surratt has worked at an auto body shop and for an inner-city youth program. What he's learned is that he would not last in a job in which he'd have to sit still and do the same thing all day. Instead, Surratt is at his best when he can "interact with people, be creative, move around to different places, and learn new things."

David Neeleman also found it hard to sit still and took off in a career that utilized his restless creative energy. Neeleman, 45, who was diagnosed with ADD about six years ago, was tired of getting to the airport and finding he'd lost his ticket. He channeled his creative energy into inventing Open Skies, the world's first "ticketless" system, and the forerunner of all the e-ticket systems used today. He went on to be the founder of the airline company Jet-Blue. Today, Neeleman often talks about his experience with ADD and links it to his success in business. "If I could take a magic pill that would get rid of it, I wouldn't," he told USA Today.

"Having a job that interests and engages you is important for everyone," says clinical psychologist Dr. Kathleen Nadeau, author of ADD in the Workplace. "But it is critical for people with ADD, because they have much less voluntary control over their attention." People with ADD have real trouble doing the work in a job that doesn't engage their interest. "But if they find something they really love," says Nadeau, "they bring an intense focus to the work and can become top employees."

In fact, says Nadeau, "many ADD traits that were problems in school can become assets on the job." Students who talked too much or couldn't sit still can, she says, find jobs where their "talkative, energetic, enthusiastic" personalities are just what the boss wants!

A Lawyer with ADD Thinks on His Feet

New York lawyer Robert Tudisco, whose ADD wasn't identified until he was 34, says teens and young adults like Rob Surratt are lucky. Already aware of having ADD, they've got a head start at

David Neeleman, pictured, was diagnosed with ADD when he was thirty-nine years old.

developing strategies that will help them succeed at work and in life. Tudisco wishes he'd been diagnosed before he "hit a brick wall" trying to handle the paperwork and billing of his law practice.

When he was diagnosed with ADD, Tudisco felt "relief" to know there was a reason why he'd always felt different. And while the challenges can be frustrating, he says ADD can be a gift—especially during a trial. "That's when I appreciate the advantages," he says. "I need the sharpness and flexibility ADD brings, that ability to respond quickly in a crisis. In court, those things are real assets to me."

Turning Struggles into Success

In her California production studio, actress and commercial voice-over artist Lora Cain remembers struggling through school before she was diagnosed with ADD. "In fourth grade, all I wanted to be was like Carla, the other red-haired girl in my class," Cain says. "Carla could sit quietly, do her work, and not make the teacher mad. Even in 12th grade, I was still being put out in the hallway for talking in class!"

After studying journalism in college, Cain found a job writing commercials at a radio station. Once the station manager heard her throaty voice, he put her on the air. "I was very good at doing five things at once—that was the ADD—so working on-air was great," Cain remembers. She was happy that somebody would pay her "to talk all day—which is what I do easily and naturally."

Eventually, Cain opened her own production studio, where she does commercial voice-over work. She has been the "voice" of Subaru and Wrangler jeans. "I get to have a lot of choice in the work I do," she says. These days, she adds, when the paperwork starts stacking up, "I hire somebody to come help me sort it out!"

If you have ADD, how can you find a career that will work for you? And how can you ensure success on the job? *Career World* asked the experts.

Planning a Career

Follow your interests, not someone else's. People with ADD too often try to live up to job expectations from their families or society by going after high-status jobs. "But if their heart isn't in it, it won't work" notes pioneering ADD therapist and writer Lynn Weiss.

ADD-Friendly Careers

What makes a job "ADD-friendly"? In Thom Hartmann's book, *ADD Success Stories*, career counselor Sharon Levine says, "People with ADD require the stimulation of changing environments, multiple responsibilities, and the ability to be responsible for their own work." ADD-friendly jobs, she says, give a worker some chance to be creative, to move around during the day, and to work independently.

- **Sales**
- **Law and law enforcement**
- **Performing arts**
- **Visual arts and design**
- **Entrepreneurship** (running your own business)
- **Teaching**
- **Counseling and therapy**
- **Recreation, fitness, sports**
- **Communications** (journalism, radio, TV, public relations)
- **"Caring" professions** (nursing, social work)
- **Culinary field** (chef, cook)

Taken from: Jan Farrington, "A.D.D. on the Job," *Career World*, vol. 34, no. 3, November/December 2005.

Sample your options. Young adults with ADD might consider taking time between high school and college to "poke around, work different jobs, and find out what interests them," suggests Weiss. Sampling, she says, often sparks a career interest.

Look for hands-on training. Learning by doing works best, says ADD coach Jodi Sleeper-Triplett. Look for high school classes with a lab or workshop component and for colleges offering work-study or co-op programs that let you work for credit while you're in school. Volunteer work and internships can spark job ideas too. A summer internship in Washington, D.C., helped Surratt know he wanted to work with at-risk teens.

Challenge yourself. Even if you've had a tough time in school, don't assume college or other high-powered training courses aren't for you. "College was actually easier for me than high school, and law school was better still, because it played to my strong points," notes Tudisco. "And in college, you are involved in a course of study that interests *you*."

On the Job

Set up a system right away. "A new, empty work space often lets you feel it's OK to just collect papers for a while," says ADD coach Sandy Maynard. "It's important to get organized before you're in trouble." Surratt, for example, "color codes" materials for each class or project and uses a big wall calendar to give himself visual reminders of what he needs to do.

Use coping strategies. Do whatever you need to do to get your job done. Tudisco wears earplugs when he has to concentrate on reading, and plays Mozart to block out distracting office noise.

Ask for what you need. You don't have to tell an employer you have ADD, says Weiss. Instead, she suggests saying, "This what I need to do my best work for you." If you have to share an office, ask to be paired with someone quiet who doesn't talk on the phone all day. If you need to come in early to have quiet time for paperwork, make that arrangement.

Look for mentors, coaches, and other support people. Many people with ADD learn best when someone shows them how to do something. Try to create informal mentoring relationships at work, Weiss suggests. Paying for an ADD coach isn't cheap, but it can work for people who need extra support. "A good ADD coach should be your partner, helping you identify and build on your strengths," says ADD coach Nancy Ratey, coauthor of *Tales from the Workplace*. Look for someone with specific experience working with clients who have ADD.

If you mess up, learn from it. "Be resilient," says Ratey. "Learn from mistakes instead of blaming yourself." And keep a sense of humor. Tudisco says he tries to turn his goof-ups into "funny stories I can tell later."

Keep your home life organized. "You are the CEO of your household," says Maynard. "Get organized about eating, exercising, paying bills, and filing papers you need to keep, and you won't have personal hassles that affect you at work."

Don't be afraid to switch jobs. If a job brings out your weaknesses instead of your strengths, make a change. "Within one career field, there are many different kinds of jobs," Nadeau says. She recalls a young social worker who was spending all day helping people fill out forms. When he found a job where he could interact with teens in a psychiatric hospital, she says, "he became a star employee, because he was operating out of his strengths."

Adding It All Up

As a college junior, Rob Surratt is thinking about ways to use his communication skills and his ADD "talents" in his future work.

"I used to see [ADD] as a disability," he says. "But now I see it as a gift. I'm creative and energetic. I come up with great ideas. I don't know where I'm going, but I know it's going to be about telling kids not to give up."

What You Should Know About ADHD

The Prevalence of ADHD

Attention deficit hyperactivity disorder (ADHD) is one of the more common mental disorders in children.

According to the Centers for Disease Control and Prevention:

- As of 2006 at least 4.5 million children and teens ages five to seven had received ADHD diagnoses.
- Approximately 3 to 7 percent of all school-aged children have ADHD, according to some studies. Other studies estimate higher rates in particular communities.
- Parental reporting is even higher, with 7.8 percent of school-aged children reported by their parents in 2003 as having been diagnosed with ADHD.
- From 1997 to 2006 the ADHD diagnosis increased an average of 3 percent every year.
- Girls are less likely than boys to have been diagnosed with ADHD (5.9 percent versus 9.5 percent).
- Boys from poor families are much more likely to be diagnosed with ADHD. The same is not true for girls.
- Non-Hispanic, primarily English-speaking, insured children are much more likely to receive an ADHD diagnosis.

ADHD Types and Diagnosis

According to the *Diagnostic and Statistical Manual of Mental Disorders* (*DSM-IV-TR*), there are three types of ADHD:

- Attention deficit hyperactivity disorder, predominantly inattentive, can be diagnosed if six or more inattention symptoms have been present for more than six months.

- Attention deficit hyperactivity disorder, predominantly hyperactive-impulse type, can be diagnosed if six or more hyperactivity-impulse symptoms have been present for more than six months.
- Attention deficit hyperactivity disorder, combined type, can be diagnosed if six or more inattention symptoms and six or more hyperactivity-impulse symptoms have been present for more than six months. Most children and teens have the combined type, but not enough study has been done to know if this is also true for adults with ADHD.

The Symptoms of ADHD

According to the *DSM-IV-TR*, a person experiencing inattention symptoms
- often makes careless mistakes or does not pay careful attention to details in schoolwork or other work;
- often has trouble paying attention during school, play, or work;
- often has trouble paying attention during conversations;
- often has difficulty following directions or finishing schoolwork or other work, but not because instructions were not understood or because of defiance;
- often has trouble organizing assignments or work;
- often procrastinates about doing work that requires sustained attention;
- often misplaces schoolwork or school or work supplies;
- is easily distracted;
- is often forgetful.

According to the *DSM-IV-TR*, a person experiencing hyperactivity symptoms
- often has trouble sitting still or keeping hands or feet still;
- often has trouble staying in his or her seat at school or in other situations;
- often runs or climbs in situations where it is not appropriate;
- often has trouble playing quietly;

- is often "on the go";
- often talks too much.

According to the *DSM-IV-TR*, a person experiencing impulsivity symptoms

- often has trouble waiting to answer questions until they have been completed;
- often has trouble waiting to take turns;
- often interrupts conversations or activities of others.

Coexisting Conditions with ADHD

According to the National Institute of Mental Health (NIMH), many people with ADHD have other conditions as well. Co-occurring conditions may include the following:

- Anxiety and/or depression
- Bipolar disorder
- Tourette's syndrome or tic disorders
- Conduct disorder
- Oppositional defiant disorder
- Learning disabilities
- Sleep disorders

The Causes of ADHD

According to the Mayo Clinic, the following may be causes of ADHD:

- Heredity: About one-quarter of all people with ADHD have at least one family member with ADHD.
- Brain disorders: The structure of the brain may be different or the part of the brain that controls attention and activity may be less active.
- Prenatal exposure to toxins: This includes tobacco smoke, drugs, alcohol, and environmental toxins.
- Childhood exposure to toxins: This includes the above, but exposure to lead or to polychlorinated biphenyls— toxic environmental pollutants—in infancy is especially a risk factor.

- Food additives and preservatives: There is no evidence that food additives are a direct cause of ADHD, but some evidence exists that certain food additives or preservatives may cause or worsen hyperactive behavior in some children.

Treatments for ADHD

According to the U.S. Department of Education, although there is no cure for ADHD, several approaches to treatment exist: behavioral, medicinal, and multimodal.

- Behavioral approaches: A wide variety of specific interventions can provide daily structure or can change the social or physical environment, all leading to positive changes in the behaviors of someone with ADHD. Parents, behavioral therapists, school personnel, and doctors can all take part in behavioral therapies, with approaches including child-management training for teachers and parents, psychotherapy, and cognitive behavioral treatment, which includes things like self-monitoring and developing strategies for problem solving.
- Medicinal approaches: Medicine is the most common treatment for ADHD. It is also the most controversial. Most commonly prescribed are stimulants such as methylphenidate (Ritalin) and dextroamphetamine (Dexedrine). Other types of medications—antidepressants, anti-anxiety medications, antipsychotics, and mood stabilizers—are usually prescribed only if stimulant medications do not work or are not appropriate due to other conditions that the patient has.
- Multimodal approaches: According to research by the NIMH, using a combination of approaches is the most effective way to treat ADHD for many people. Hundreds of children with ADHD were followed and four treatments compared: behavioral, medicinal, behavioral and medicinal, and no-intervention community care. Of the four, the combination of behavior therapy and medicine was the most effective.

The Future of Treatment for ADHD

According to PsychCentral, although no cure for ADHD is on the horizon, new information about ADHD is being discovered.

- Using improved brain-imaging techniques, scientists are better able to understand how the brain functions and what is going wrong when ADHD is present. The more that they understand about what causes ADHD, the better they can tailor the treatments.
- Researchers are also trying to pinpoint differing kinds of ADHD so they can offer more specific treatment options.
- Other research is focusing on childhood and prebirth causes of ADHD.
- Nonstimulant medications are being developed for the treatment of ADHD.

What You Should Do About ADHD

Understand ADHD and Be Understanding

Whether you have ADHD or have a family member or friend with the disorder, it is important to understand the basic nature of it. First of all, realize that it is a real neurobiological medical condition. A person does not have ADHD symptoms like inattentiveness or trouble sitting still in class because he or she is bad or because of inadequate parenting. Neither are people with ADHD lazy or lacking intelligence. ADHD is an emotionally painful and frustrating condition; shaming or making fun of someone with ADHD only makes it worse for the person who is already suffering.

Secondly, understand that although there is no cure for ADHD, it is a treatable condition. Many medical professionals do believe that medication, if taken consistently, helps most people with ADHD, as do certain types of therapy, and a combination of medication and therapy seems to help the most. Therefore, if you have ADHD, do your research, consult with respected professionals, and precisely follow their instructions.

Use Coping Techniques

For those who have ADHD, in addition to taking medication and seeking therapy, employing certain strategies can help you manage your life and your ADHD symptoms:

- Find things that calm you: deep breathing, closing your eyes, squeezing a ball, writing in a journal, and so on.
- Write things down; take a lot of notes in class.
- Carry an organizer, and use it.
- Make lists, and focus on accomplishing one task at a time. Break down large tasks into smaller ones.
- Prepare for the next day the night before.

- Stick to a schedule.
- Get enough rest.

Exercise Your Rights

Whether you are in grade school, middle school, high school, or college, an ADHD diagnosis guarantees you certain rights under the Individuals with Disabilities Education Act (IDEA). One of these rights is an Individualized Education Plan (IEP), written by your teacher in conjunction with your parents and educational specialists at your school. An IEP will identify your specific educational needs and outline a plan with short-term goals for meeting those needs. The goals should be specific, measurable, and achievable. You are also entitled to receive special education services, if deemed necessary, to achieve these goals.

To get an IEP you will first need an ADHD diagnosis, and you and a parent will need to meet with teachers and school specialists. Your parent may need to be persistent about making this happen and making sure that your IEP really does meet your needs. Many of the organizations listed in the Organizations to Contact section of this book offer helpful suggestions regarding working with schools.

Choose a College Carefully

If you have ADHD and are looking at colleges, there are many things to consider. First of all, does the Student Disability Services department have specialists on staff that have experience with students with ADHD? What kind of support services do they offer for students with ADHD? Possibilities include support groups, study-skills programs, ADHD coaches, advocates who will help you get the accommodations that you need from instructors, and physicians on campus who can manage your ADHD medications. Also consider class sizes. Students with ADHD may do better in a smaller class with more individualized attention and more opportunities to participate and to ask questions. Finally, consider living arrangements. If a single room or living at home or off-campus is critical to your success in college, make sure those options are available to you.

Respect Prescription Medications

The majority of ADHD sufferers who are treated with medication are prescribed stimulants, such as Ritalin. Unfortunately, abuse of these medications, both for performance enhancement by students and for recreational purposes, is a growing problem not only on high school and college campuses but also in elementary and middle schools. The danger of abusing these medications cannot be overstated. Not only is addiction a real possibility, but paranoia, cardiac problems, strokes and even death may result. If you are prescribed medications for ADHD management, it is very important that you take them as prescribed. Sharing them with or selling them to others is not only illegal and punishable by law, but it also poses extreme hazards. If you know someone with ADHD, respect his or her medications. Do not share them.

Get Involved

One of the most important things that you should do concerning ADHD is be proactive—get involved and take action. If someone is bullying or making fun of classmates with ADHD, stand up for them and be considerate of them yourself. If you have ADHD, learn as much as you can about the disorder and do whatever you can to help others understand it as well. You can start with the bibliography in this book. Also, seek out the organizations listed in the Organizations to Contact section of this book. Sign up for newsletters and other publications that they offer, and look into the online support groups that they facilitate or local support groups that they might list.

You can also enlist your own support team, including your family and friends. Be open and honest with them about what it is like to have ADHD and how it affects you. If you feel like you need accommodations at school, talk to your parents and insist that they have you evaluated by a physician for ADHD, if you have not been yet, and that they speak with your teachers.

Lobby for more ADHD support services at your school. Write a letter, start a letter-writing campaign, visit a school board meeting, or simply verbally request things like ADHD coaches, support groups for students and parents, or ADHD magazines and books for the school library.

Finally, start an ADHD public awareness campaign at your school. With the permission of your school administration, make posters or distribute information about the symptoms of ADHD, facts about ADHD, and the dangers of abusing ADHD medications. If you have a persuasive or information speech or research paper assignment, use that as an opportunity to think, write, and talk about an aspect of ADHD.

ORGANIZATIONS TO CONTACT

The editors have compiled the following list of organizations concerned with the issues debated in this book. The descriptions are derived from materials provided by the organizations. All have publications or information available for interested readers. The list was compiled on the date of publication of the present volume; names, addresses, phone and fax numbers, and e-mail and Internet addresses may change. Be aware that many organizations take several weeks or longer to respond to inquiries, so allow as much time as possible.

American Academy of Child and Adolescent Psychiatry (AACAP)
3615 Wisconsin Ave. NW, Washington, DC 20016-3007
phone: (202) 966-7300
fax: (202) 966-2891
e-mail: communications@aacap.org
Web site: www.aacap.org

The AACAP is a member-based professional organization composed of more than seventy-five hundred child and adolescent psychiatrists and other interested physicians. It widely distributes information in an effort to assure proper treatment and access to services for children and adolescents. It publishes the parenting guides *Your Child* and *Your Adolescent*, fact sheets for families, informational videos, and a glossary of symptoms and mental illnesses.

American Psychiatric Association (APA)
1000 Wilson Blvd., Ste. 1825, Arlington, VA 22209-3901
phone: (703) 907-7300
e-mail: apa@psych.org
Web site: www.psych.org

An organization of psychiatrists dedicated to studying the nature, treatment, and prevention of mental disorders, the APA helps create mental health policies, distributes information about psychiatry, and promotes psychiatric research and education. It publishes the *American Journal of Psychiatry* and *Psychiatric News Monthly*.

American Psychological Association
750 First St. NE, Washington, DC 20002-4242
phone: (202) 336-5500
e-mail: public.affairs@apa.org
Web site: www.apa.org

This professional organization for psychologists aims to advance psychology as a science, as a profession, and as a means of promoting human welfare. It produces the journal *American Psychologist* as well as numerous publications available online, including the monthly newsletters *Monitor on Psychology*.

Attention Deficit Disorder Association (ADDA)
PO Box 7557, Wilmington, DE 19803-9997
phone: (856) 439-9099 or (800) 939-1019
e-mail: info@add.org
Web site: www.add.org

The goal of ADDA is to generate hope, awareness, empowerment, and connections for adults with ADHD. It provides information, resources, and networking opportunities through its Web site, publications, and conferences. Publications include articles on ADHD diagnosis and management, a support group manual, and a database of ADHD professionals.

Attention Deficit Disorder Resources
223 Tacoma Ave. S., Ste. 100, Tacoma, WA 98402
phone: (253) 759-5085
fax: (253) 572-3700
email: office@addresources.org
Web site: www.addresources.org

The goal of Attention Deficit Disorder Resources is to help individuals with ADHD reach their full potential through education and support. Its Web site provides some articles for free. For members who pay a nominal fee, it provides additional articles; *ADDult ADDvice*, a quarterly newsletter; and a lending library of books, audio, and video. It also provides online teleconferences as well as teacher workshops and a social networking site for people with ADHD.

Centers for Disease Control and Prevention (CDC)
National Center for Injury Prevention and Control
4770 Buford Hwy. NE, MS F-63, Atlanta, GA 30341-3717
phone: (800) 232-4636
fax: (770) 488-4760
e-mail: cdcinfo@cdc.gov
Web site: www.cdc.gov/ncbddd/adhd

The CDC is dedicated to protecting health and promoting quality of life through the prevention and control of disease, injury, and disability. The CDC is committed to programs that reduce the health and economic consequences of the leading causes of death and disability. Fact sheets, reports, statistics, and podcasts are available on its Web site.

Children and Adults with Attention-Deficit/Hyperactivity Disorder (CHADD)
8181 Professional Pl., Ste. 150, Landover, MD 20785
phone: (301) 306-7070 or (800) 233-4050
Web site: www.chadd.org

CHADD provides support and information for individuals with ADHD and their families, with local chapters offering support for individuals, parents, teachers, and other professionals. Publications include the bimonthly member magazine *Attention!* CHADD also sponsors an annual conference and the National Resource Center on AD/HD (NRC), a CDC-funded national clearinghouse for evidence-based information about ADHD. The NRC includes a searchable library of articles, fact sheets, and information on educational and legal rights of individuals with ADHD.

National Center for Girls and Women with AD/HD
3268 Arcadia Pl. NW, Washington, DC 20015
e-mail: contact@ncgiadd.org
Web site: www.ncgiadd.org

This organization exists to promote awareness, advocacy, and research on ADHD in women and girls. It sponsors a virtual conference and offers information on its Web site such as articles, a multimedia library, and a listing of support groups for women with ADHD.

National Center for Learning Disabilities (NCLD)
381 Park Ave. S., Ste. 1401, New York, NY 10016
phone: (212) 545-7510 or (888) 575-7373
fax: (212) 545-9665
e-mail: ncld@ncld.org
Web site: www.ncld.org

The NCLD works to ensure that children, adolescents, and adults with learning disabilities have equal opportunities to succeed in school, work, and life. The NCLD produces publications, including a quarterly newsletter, *LD Essentials*, and a monthly newsletter, *LD News*. Through its Web site it provides advocacy guides, policy-related publications, checklists, work sheets, and forms.

National Institute of Mental Health (NIMH)
6001 Executive Blvd., Bethesda, MD 20892
phone: (866) 615-6464 or (301) 443-4513
fax: (301) 443-4279
e-mail: nimhinfo@nih.gov
Web site: www.nimh.nih.gov

The mission of NIMH is to transform the understanding and treatment of mental illnesses through basic and clinical research, paving the way for prevention, recovery, and cure. NIMH publishes brochures, fact sheets, and educational curricula. Videos of selected NIMH-sponsored lectures, conferences, and presentations are available for online viewing.

BIBLIOGRAPHY

Books

Lenard Adler, *Scattered Minds: Hope and Help for Adults with Attention Deficit Hyperactivity Disorder*. New York: G.P. Putnam's Sons, 2006.

Susan Ashley, *The ADD & ADHD Answer Book*. Naperville, IL: Sourcebooks, 2005.

Russell A. Barkley, *Attention-Deficit Hyperactivity Disorder: A Handbook for Diagnosis and Treatment*. 3rd ed. New York: Guilford, 2006.

Shirley Brinkerhoff, *Stuck on Fast Forward: Youth with Attention-Deficit/Hyperactivity Disorder*. Broomall, PA: Mason Crest, 2004.

Pamela J. Compart, *The Kid-Friendly ADHD & Autism Cookbook: The Ultimate Guide to the Gluten-Free, Milk-Free Diet*. 2nd ed. Beverly, MA: Fair Winds, 2009.

Stanley I. Greenspan, *Overcoming ADHD: Helping Your Child Become Calm, Engaged, and Focused—Without a Pill*. Cambridge, MA: Da Capo/Lifelong, 2009.

Frank Jacobelli, *ADD/ADHD Drug Free: Natural Alternatives and Practical Exercises to Help Your Child Focus*. New York: AMACOM/American Management Association, 2008.

Gwynedd Lloyd, Joan Stead, and David Cohen, eds., *Critical New Perspectives on ADHD*. New York: Routledge, 2006.

Francha Roffé Menhard, *The Facts About Ritalin*. New York: Marshall Cavendish Benchmark, 2006.

Jonas Pomere, *Frequently Asked Questions About ADD and ADHD*. New York: Rosen, 2007.

Patricia O. Quinn, *Putting on the Brakes: Understanding and Taking Control of Your ADD and ADHD*. Washington, DC: Imagination, 2009.

John K. Rosemond, *The Diseasing of America's Children: Exposing the ADHD Fiasco and Empowering Parents to Take Back Control*. Nashville: Thomas Nelson, 2008.

Blake E.S. Taylor, *ADHD and Me: What I Learned from Lighting Fires at the Dinner Table*. Oakland, CA: New Harbinger, 2007.

John F. Taylor, *The Survival Guide for Kids with ADD or ADHD*. Minneapolis: Free Spirit, 2006.

Peg Tyre, *The Trouble with Boys: A Surprising Report Card on Our Sons, Their Problems at School, and What Parents and Educators Must Do*. New York: Crown, 2008.

Periodicals

Linda Bernstein, "ADHD Nation," *Current Health 2*, Fall 2006.

Bruce Bower, "Attention Disorder Has Lasting Impact on Girls," *Science News*, July 8, 2006.

———, "ADHD Drug's Mental Lift Proves Surprisingly Weak," *Science News*, November 3, 2007.

Oscar G. Bukstein, "Substance Use Disorders in Patients with ADHD: Risk Factors and Prevention," *Psychiatric Times*, Summer 2007 supplement.

William Dodson, "ADHD: Not Just a Childhood Disorder," *EP*, October 2008.

Theresa Lavoie, "Introduction and Overview to ADHD," *EP*, March 2008.

Karl E. Miller, "Relationship Between Smoking and ADHD Behaviors," *American Family Physician*, May 2006.

Daniel S. Pine, "Editorial: Evaluating New and Old Treatments for ADHD," *Journal of Child Psychology and Psychiatry*, July 2009.

Margaret Talbot, "Brain Gain: The Underground World of 'Neuroenhancing' Drugs," *New Yorker*, April 27, 2009.

Patrick Tucker, "Curing 'Nature Deficit Disorder,'" *Futurist*, May/June 2006.

Debra Viadero, "Computer Training Found to Help Those with ADHD," *Education Week*, June 6, 2007.

———, "ADHD Experts Fear Brain-Growth Study Being Misconstrued," *Education Week*, December 5, 2007.

Perry A. Zirkel, "No Med, No Ed?" *Phi Delta Kappan*, February 2007.

Internet Sources

Mike Adams and Fred Baughman, "Live with Dr. Fred Baughman: ADHD Fraud and the Chemical Holocaust Against a Generation of Children," Truth, 2006. http://downloads.truth publishing.com/LivewithFredBaughman.pdf.

Megan Johnson, "9 Drug-Free Approaches to Managing ADHD: Meditation and 8 Other Treatment Techniques That May Ease ADHD Symptoms," *U.S. News & World Report Online*, August 12, 2009. www.usnews.com/health/family-health/ brain-and-behavior/articles/2009/08/12/9-drug-free-approaches-to-managing-adhd.html.

National Institute on Drug Abuse, "Stimulant ADHD Medications: Methylphenidate and Amphetamines," *NIDA Info-Facts*, June 2009. www.drugabuse.gov.

ScienceDaily, "ADHD Genes Found, Known to Play Roles in Neurodevelopment," June 24, 2009. www.sciencedaily.com/ releases/ 2009/06/090623120835.htm.

Nancy Shute, "ADHD Medication: Can Your Child Go Without? Behavioral Therapy for ADHD—and Parent Retraining, Too—Can Be Good Alternatives to Medication," *U.S. News & World Report Online*, January 14, 2009. www.usnews.com/ health/family-health/brain-and-behavior/articles/2009/01/14/ adhd-medication-can-your-child-go-without.html.

U.S. Department of Health and Human Services Public Health Service, "What Causes AD/HD?" www.add.org/articles/cause add.html.

INDEX

A

ADD in the Workplace (Nadeau), 106

Adderall (amphetamine and dextroamphetamine), *67, 71,* 72–73

abuse of by students, 71–72

Canada suspends use of, 56, 73

dangers of, 74

nonmedical use of, *75*

See also Amphetamines

ADDitude (magazine), 66, 81

ADHD & Me (Taylor), 24

Adolescents. *See* Children/adolescents

Advertising, 64–68

Agency for Healthcare Research and Quality (AHRQ), 62

American Journal of Psychiatry, 52, 59

American Psychological Association, 82

Amphetamines, sudden death from, *61*

Anxiety disorders, 12–13

Archives of Pediatric and Adolescent Medicine (journal), 6

Asher, Jules, 73

Attention deficit disorder (ADD), 99

prevalence of, 105

Attention deficit hyperactivity disorder (ADHD)

academic performance and, 15–16

alternatives to drugs can help treat, 98–104

behavior therapy may prevent, 84–85

careers friendly to, *109*

causes of increase in, 92

diet can help treat, 91–97

has lost much of its stigma, 22–29

home functioning and, 16–17

link between Internet addiction and, 6–8

other conditions occurring with, 11–14

people with, 105–111

percent of children diagnosed with, *23, 65*

percent of children medicated for, *33*

prevalence of, 47, 64

problems among youth with/without, *15*

social functioning and, 16

in teens *vs.* children, 10–11

Autism, 91–92

Sleep disturbance, 13
Sleeper-Triplett, Jodi, 110
Soy, 94
Stephens, Joe, 101
Stimulants
  effects on growth, 41
  sudden death associated
    with, 60
  See also Amphetamines;
    Methylphenidate
Strattera, 56
Stump, Mary Katherine, 71–72
Substance abuse
  ADHD drugs do not increase
    risk of, 46–52
  among men treated/not
    treated by stimulants, *50*
  risk for, 13
Sudden death, *61*
  and stimulant use, 60
Surratt, Rob, 105–106, 111
Swanson, James, 52, 85

T
Tales from the Workplace
  (Ratey), 111
Taylor, Blake, 24–26, 27,
  28–29
Teachers, 88–89
Todd, Richard D., 36–37, 38, 39

Treatment
  of ADHD is not consistent,
    34
  ADHD symptoms after, *42*
  fewer girls with ADHD
    receive, 39
  importance of education as
    part of, 17–18
  percent of children with
    ADHD seeking, 38
  See also Behavior therapy;
    Behavioral treatments;
    Medications, ADHD
Tudisco, Robert, 106–108

V
Volkow, Nora, 52

W
Washington University
  School of Medicine, 35
Weber, Wendy, 92, 93, 97
Weiss, Lynn, 108

Y
Young, Kimberly S., 5

Z
Zinc deficiency, 95–96, 96
Zwerdling, David, 73–74

PICTURE CREDITS